# paedofaith:
## a primer on the mystery of infant salvation and a handbook for covenant parents

rich lusk

athanasius press
monroe, louisiana

Rich Lusk
Paedofaith: *A Primer on the Mystery of Infant Salvation and a Handbook for Covenant Parents*
© 2005

Published by Athanasius Press
205 Roselawn
Monroe, LA 71201
318-323-3061

paedofaith:
*a primer on the mystery of infant salvation*
*and a handbook for covenant parents*

# preface and dedication

Faithful Christian parenting is hard work. Every child presents his or her own distinctive challenges and difficulties. Every child will have his or her unique ups and downs, triumphs and defeats, joys and struggles, and phases and stages. Nothing can prepare parents for everything they will face. There is no possibility of taking a cookie-cutter approach. Every child is full of mystery and possibility.

Living at the end of an era further complicates the parenting task. The capital of medieval and Reformational Christendom is nearly spent, and a new dark age of moral bankruptcy is upon us. This is a time of transition, but to an era of we-know-not-what. Our period seems more "catacomb" than "cathedral," more "exile" than "conquest" for the faithful remnant in the West. Christian moms and dads in twenty-first century America have all the powerful forces of worldly culture arrayed against them, seeking to undermine their efforts at every step. A new temptation for our children is lurking right around every corner, aiming to suck them into crass hedonism, materialism, consumerism, or some other pattern of vice that afflicts our sick, idolatrous civilization. Our culture hates maturity and basks in ignorance. The ubiquity of pop culture makes retreatist, isolationist strategies naïve. We cannot merely build a hedge around our homes to keep the world out. We have to train and equip our children to face and fight the world in all its worldliness, rather than seek to escape from it. It seems that we confront very long odds as we aim at inculcating wisdom, discipline, habitual holiness, and a missional spirit in our children, living as we do in a (post)modern world of faithlessness and flux.

In such circumstances, we must ask, is there any biblical constant we can rely on in raising our children? The answer to that question is most assuredly, *Yes.* That constant is the covenant. God's covenant with us is utterly trustworthy, and it includes our children. The covenant is the bedrock on which we seek to build our own lives and the lives of our children. The covenant does not make parenting a simple task, but it does provide a framework for understanding who our children are, what we should do for them, and what we should expect from them.

Grasping the way in which our children participate by grace through faith in God's covenant is the heart of faithful Christian parenting—and the heart of this book as well. In light of the covenant promises, Christian parents must press upon their children the privileges and obligations of covenant membership, training them to recognize and regard themselves as children of God, so that they will feel, think, and act accordingly.

My hope is that this book—which focuses especially on how the promises of God to our children apply even from the point of conception—will help Christian parents undertake their task with greater faithfulness and diligence. God's covenant promises embrace our children at every stage of their development, from the commencement of life forward. Of course, God's gracious gift does not eliminate the possibility of presumption or even apostasy later in life; therefore, we must be vigilant as parents, and exhort our children to vigilance as well. We teach our children to repent continually and believe precisely because we believe they are *already* believers. If the church is going to thrive in a post-Christendom situation, she must do a much better job of keeping her children true to the faith of their childhood. We must not wait to begin Spiritually nurturing our children, or we will always be playing catch-up in our quest to form mature disciples of Christ. We must recover the principles and methods of covenant succession. This book is my humble contribution to that end.

I offer special thanks to the board of Athanasius Press for supporting the publication of this book. There have been very, very few published works on the topic of infant faith in Reformed circles, and only a handful more by Lutheran and Anglican theologians. The subject is often ignored, ridiculed, or relegated to minimal treatment as a subsidiary of discussions about infant baptism. I know of no book-length treatment on infant faith in print in English. Only a few articles on the subject exist and even fewer are readily available. Nevertheless, the Athanasius board was willing to allow this rather odd piece of work to see the light of day, and for that I am grateful. I hope their risk will be amply rewarded. I trust this volume will fill an important but empty niche on Reformed bookshelves.

Duane and Sarah Garner deserve heaps of praise for handling the technical aspects of publication, including editing and indexing. Without their efforts, this book would never have made it off my hard drive and to the printer. The Garners have continually performed invaluable, behind-the-scenes work for Athanasius Press. They deserve public credit for their hard labor and sound counsel along the way. Of course, the final product in your hands—flaws and all—remains my responsibility (God help me!).

This book is dedicated (for obvious reasons) to my family: my wife of ten years, Jenny, and our four growing paedobelievers—John, Rebekah, Hannah Kate, and Annie. Jenny has been a wonderful companion in the hard but rewarding work of raising our children. She is a faithful wife and mother, playing to perfection the most difficult role in the world, that of a pastor's wife. She models faith in the reliability of God's covenant promise to be our God and the God of our children. She is my constant joy and my greatest earthly treasure. Watching our children grow toward maturity together (physically, socially, and especially in Christ) is both thrilling and rewarding. Hopefully this book can serve as a small token of my appreciation for the lessons we have learned (and continue to learn!) together.

I trust that when my children get a bit older they may have some interest in this work. (After all, they wonder even now what Dad is doing in the basement all day long!) Well, kids, this is it: I spent hours working on this book so that you'd know what Mom and I were trying to accomplish in your lives all these years! Our goal all along has been to form your initial paedofaith into mature, humble, obedient adult faith so that you can serve loyally in Christ's kingdom all your days. Forgive us where we failed you and rejoice with us in the free grace that God has given to us as a family. And most of all, never forget my family mantras: "Remember your baptism!" and "Be who you are!"

*August 14, 2005*
*Thirteenth Sunday of Trinity Season*
*Birmingham, Alabama*

# contents

# introduction

## _the vexing question_

The question whether or not infants of Christian parents can have faith
has been a vexing one throughout the history of the church. For some
theologians, infants are the model of gospel grace because their helplessness is so utterly apparent. Not only is it affirmed that infants can
have faith, the reality is that they can have _nothing but_ faith![1] Others

---

1. The Puritan Thomas Hooker argued infants were more fit recipients of
baptism than adults because they were less habituated in sin and therefore less
prone to resist the Spirit. See E. Brooks Holifield, _The Covenant Sealed: The Development of Puritan Sacramental Theology in Old and New England, 1570–1720_ (New
Haven and London: Yale University Press, 1974). See also B. B. Warfield, "Children," in _Selected Shorter Writings_ (Phillipsburg, NJ: Presbyterian and Reformed,
reprint, 2001), vol. 1, 224ff. Warfield suggests children are models of kingdom
membership not because of their supposed innocence, or humility, or even because of their disposition to trust, but because of their utter and obvious dependence on others. It is "in a word, in the helplessness, or, if you will, the absolute
dependence of infancy" that their fitness for the kingdom is found. Infants are

view the mere suggestion of paedofaith as ridiculous, as "incompatible with Scripture and common sense."[2] Infants have not yet developed powers of mind and will, so they are incapable of exercising belief. Infant faith is an "anthropologically and psychologically impossible construction."[3] Discussion of the issue has often been clouded by poor exegesis, debatable definitions of faith, and widely varying presuppositions about the innate abilities of infants and the ways in which God works on the human mind and heart.

If faith is defined as a composite of knowledge, assent, and trust, then clearly infants do *not* have faith. They cannot have propositional knowledge and do not have the self-awareness needed for active assent; however, perhaps infants are capable of a "seed" of faith, defined here as a *relational posture of trust* toward another person.[4] There is much

---

the best illustrations of grace: "The children of the kingdom enter it as children enter the world, stripped and naked—infants, for whom all must be done, not who are capable of doing . . . As children enter the world, so men enter the kingdom, with no contributions in their hands." Their state of "utter dependence" thus reveals "the real condition of every sinner" (230–31). Children are important because of the transparent insight they give us into the human condition. Of course, they are also offensive to some for just this same reason. Arminians, of course, could never affirm paedofaith since for them, faith is a human work and requires some measure of intellectual as well as moral ability. Only Calvinists— who stress that faith is a gift of God's sovereign grace—can even contemplate the possibility of paedofaith. Many of the church fathers who advocated a doctrine of infant faith (e.g., Augustine) did so by pointing to the gift-nature of faith. The leading Reformers did the same, as we will see. In fact, many Reformers viewed infant baptism, including the gift of infant faith, as a measure of the graciousness of the gospel.

2. Paul K. Jewett, *Infant Baptism and the Covenant of Grace* (Grand Rapids: Eerdmans, 1978), 168.

3. This is the view of Werner Wiesner, quoted in Gottfried Hoffmann's essay "The Baptism and Faith of Children" in *A Lively Legacy: Essays in Honor of Robert Preus*, eds. Kurt Marquart, John R. Stephenson, and Bjarne W. Teigen (Fort Wayne, IN: Graphic Publishing Company, 1985), 83.

4. "Seed faith" in this paper is simply "baby faith." Hoffman's definition is helpful. "Faith therefore here means a confident personal relatedness of the heart to Jesus which can exist without a detailed and articulated understanding of what is and must be unfolded in the proclamation of the gospel . . . This state of affairs leads to an intensification of the concept of faith in the case of children on account of the fact that it here means a relatedness to Christ, a trust in the person of Christ behind which the individual and utterable elements of the deposit of

*prima facie* evidence in Scripture that makes such a viewpoint plausible.

The purpose of this work is to take a closer look at those biblical data (focusing on the psalms and the gospels) with the desire to draw a hard verdict about the possibility (and even probability) of infant faith. After reaching a favorable conclusion with regard to infant faith in covenant families, we will turn to deal with the question of the fate of infants who die in infancy. We will also look summarily at the historical precedents for infant faith within the Protestant tradition and seek to draw out some of the theological, pastoral, and parental implications that flow out of our affirmation of paedofaith. We will find paedofaith to be grounded in a biblical theology of the covenant promises and of immense practical significance for the life of the church.

---

faith recede. Even for adults, there obtains in principle no other way to enter the Kingdom of Heaven than for children and infants: faith in Jesus" (87).

Faith's core of relational trust matures to include propositional knowledge and mental/volitional assent as the child grows.

# paedofaith in the psalms

The Psalter is the great handbook of Christian experience. It covers the whole range of Christian feeling and devotion from infancy to old age. It climbs to the heights of God's grace and sinks to the depths of human despair. If we desire to understand our own experiences of God's grace, and those of our children, there is no better place to turn. In particular, if we want to understand what it means to grow up in a covenant family among the people of God, in the psalms we will find a rich treasury of testimony and practical instruction. Much of what we see in the Psalter with regard to the experiences of the faithful surprises us. We find David (and others) saying things we would never dare say. Nowhere is this more true than when it comes to covenant children. The Psalter gives us a very different view of growing up in the covenant than one finds in the great bulk of American Christianity (even in its Reformed expressions).[1]

---

1. Obviously, this is troubling. Unfortunately, the historic Reformed practice of singing psalms in worship has been undercut by contemporary worship music. While this newer music is not sinful, of course, it is often trite and shallow

## Psalm 22

We begin our survey with Psalm 22. In Psalm 22:9–10, David asserts that he had faith as an infant. He sees continuity between the faith he possesses now as an adult and the faith he had as a child, even in the womb. He explains that he had a Godward orientation from his earliest days. In recounting his formative experiences, David never points to a dramatic "conversion experience," but always traces back the origin of his Spiritual life to the very beginnings of his physical life. As far as David knows, a relationship with God was always already there. He passed through no preparatory phase on his way to becoming a faithful covenant member; he did not have to wait until he reached an age of accountability to become a believer; he did not have to be able to articulate propositional truth in order to exercise faith.

David claims to have had paedofaith (that is, infant faith). This was certainly *not* because David believed infants somehow escaped the pollution of original sin or possessed an innate moral goodness. David was not a naïve sentimentalist or a proto-Pelagian. In fact, David confesses elsewhere that he was conceived in iniquity (Ps. 51:5). Apparently, for David, sin and faith were no more mutually exclusive in infants than in adults. Humans are sinners from the moment of conception, yet in those infants who are also participants in the covenant promises, God's grace is already operative.

Those who claim *a priori* that infant faith is impossible pose several alternative readings of Psalm 22:9–10, of course. Perhaps, they say, this portion of the psalm is Christological, not Davidic. They will point to other explicitly messianic portions of the psalm (22:1, 22:14ff). This is based on a flawed hermeneutic. The entire psalm—indeed, *the entire Psalter*—is messianic (e.g., Lk. 24:44; cf. Rom. 15:3; Heb. 10:5). Psalm 22 is both historical and Christological. It is a prayer of David *and* a prayer of Jesus. Indeed, Jesus prayed it *through* David as His prototype and

---

compared to the psalms and hymns shaped by the psalms. It cannot bring us to the same level of maturity as the singing of psalms. As we have lost touch with the Psalter, we have lost touch with our best model for a life of piety and devotion. We need to put the psalms back at the center of corporate worship. Until we do so, many biblical themes (including paedofaith, as I will argue here) will seem completely foreign to us.

forerunner.[2] But we cannot discount the meaning of this psalm in its original context, nor can we carve up the psalm into sections that belong exclusively to David and sections that belong solely to Jesus. However prophetic they may be of the coming Christ, these are David's own words, penned under inspiration, describing his own life.[3] David's case is a *bona fide*, irrefutable example of paedofaith.

Others have suggested that David's words are not to be taken at face value in their literal sense. In other words, David is not actually saying he *remembers* having faith as an infant; rather, he is using poetic license to make a point about God's care for him from early on in life. This is David's typical, exaggerated way of describing the overwhelming goodness of God. Elsewhere the psalm uses poetic language to describe David's enemies as wild beasts (e.g., 22:12, 16); perhaps the description of infant faith should be interpreted metaphorically as well.

Certainly, I do not think we need to say that David *consciously remembers* trusting in God, even from the womb. Obviously, none of us can remember that far back in our experience! But in reality, this only strengthens the case for infant faith. David is asserting that he had faith, and he *knows* he had faith. This is not simply hyperbolic, poetic lan-

---

2. On the pervasive Christology of the book of Psalms, see James E. Adams, *War Psalms of the Prince of Peace* (Phillipsburg, NJ: Presbyterian and Reformed, 1991).

3. Of course, even if we limited the words to Christ, we would still have an example of infant faith. Jesus Himself was fully human; if He was capable of faith as an infant, in principle, other infants are capable of faith as well. We must reject docetic christologies, even when contemplating Jesus' infancy. He is like us in every way (including the capacity for faith) except sin. We might ask, assuming that Jesus is the ultimate Man of Faith (Heb. 12:1–2), *at what age did He begin to trust His heavenly Father?* To ask the question is to answer it. Surely the human Jesus never lived without faith, even as an embryo. John Calvin writes: "Truly Christ was sanctified from earliest infancy in order that He might sanctify in Himself His elect from every age without distinction . . . If we have in Christ the most perfect example of all the graces which God bestows upon His children, in this respect also He will be for us a proof that the age of infancy is not utterly averse to sanctification" (*Institutes of the Christian Religion*, trans. Ford Lewis Battles [Philadelphia: Westminster Press, 1960], 4.16.18).

This argument that Christ passed through each stage of human life to sanctify it goes all the way back to the early Church; however, the sanctification of life only takes place as the Spirit works faith.

guage, nor is it a matter of speculation or conjecture. David is doing more than simply saying that he cannot remember a time in his life when he did not know God (though that is included). *He is viewing his infancy through the lens of the covenant promise*, setting forth what must have been his pre-cognitive experience. David knows the covenant promise explicitly includes the children of believers: "I will establish My covenant between Me and you and your descendants after you in their generations, for an everlasting covenant, to be God to you and your descendants after you" (Gen. 17:7).

Before a child of the promise can do any good work or make any kind of profession, God is already his God. In this psalm, David narrates the early chapters of his life story not in terms of remembered experiences, but in terms of God's covenant pledge. He derives the fact that he had infant faith not from an introspective examination of his past, but from an exegesis of the covenant promises.

Thus, in light of David's claim, we can say as soon as a covenant child is conceived, the promise has validity for that child. The promise does *not* say that God will become a God to our children when they reach a certain age or level of intellectual and physical maturity; rather, the promise declares that *from the very beginning of their lives*, our children stand in the same covenantal relationship with God that we ourselves are in by virtue of faith. They participate in the faith-life of the community. In other words, the child of the covenant is not only given promises, he is given the faith by which those promises are appropriated and made his own. The covenant child is included in a faith-based covenantal relationship with God. To deny the reality of paedofaith is to say the covenant promise only stretches halfway between God and the child. It implies covenant children are automatically covenant-breakers because they cannot fulfill the covenant conditions.

In light of this psalm, we must conclude that the status and standing of children in the covenant are identical to that of their parents. The children share in the faith of their parents and thus share in the same blessings and benefits of the covenant. God is our God from the time of our youth if we are conceived and born into a covenant family.

Properly understood, this doesn't feed presumption, for while the covenant is a blessed relationship, it is also a conditional relationship

(Gen. 17:1, 8). Our children are under the same covenantal demand of persevering faith that we are under. They must mature in faith as they mature in other aspects of their personality. They must grow, even as we must we grow (cf. 1 Pt. 2:2); however, Psalm 22:9–10 describes the normative *starting point* for covenant children. God gives us children with faith. Covenant children begin life as believers, not in need of conversion but endurance (cf. Heb. 10:36). They should be received and raised as children of God.

Note that David is not presenting his paedofaith as a one-in-a-million case. After all, his description of faith, even from the womb, was part of Israel's public hymnbook used in corporate worship. This is not a private prayer journal, but part of a covenantal liturgy. In public praise, every Israelite would have made the words of David his own and would have been expected to be able to identify with them in some form or fashion. While I would not necessarily want to claim infant faith is absolutely universal among covenant children (more on this in chapter five), at the very least, we can say it is "normative" or "paradigmatic" or "expected."[4] It is the normal course of events, part of a typical covenant child's pattern of development. In much the same way that hymns like Wesley's "And Can It Be?" have made adult conversion the norm ("Long my imprisoned

---

4. It seems to me that paedofaith is even bound up in the biblical warrant for paedobaptism, a notion we shall return to near the end of this book. At this point, a few thoughts will suffice: to baptize unbelieving subjects would profane and abuse baptism just as much as inviting unbelievers to the Lord's Table would abuse the sacramental meal. We would never knowingly baptize unbelieving adults, so why baptize a child unless we have some reason to regard him as a believer? *At the very least*, infant faith should be regarded as a presumption or judgment of charity, though I think it preferable to view it as a matter of trusting the covenant promises. In an absolute sense, we can never know another's heart, so we can never know with absolute certainty if they possess faith. In this sense, regarding infants as believers is really no different than regarding professing Christian adults as genuine believers. If parents believe God's covenant promises to and about their children, I see no reason for them to doubt the presence of faith in the hearts of their children. Psalm 22:9–10 is as true of their children as it was of David. Thus, in a healthy Reformed church, there is absolutely no solid basis for doubting the faith of the little ones in the congregation. God is a God to our children; being their God entails giving them faith. He promises to become a God to them in infancy, not at some later date. Our children are not aliens and strangers to the covenant promises, but are fully included.

spirit lay . . .") in revivalistic churches, so David's psalm made infant faith and covenant nurture the norm in ancient Israel. Certainly, God is free to work when, how, and where He pleases, but God's *ordinary* way of dealing with covenant infants includes giving them the gift of faith in the womb.[5] The revivalistic paradigm turns David's experience inside out. The typical pattern is for a covenant child to grow in faith from his infancy (cf. the prophet's testimony in 1 Ki. 18:12).

Finally, why does David tie his paedofaith to nursing at his mother's breast in verse nine? It seems that David is indicating that God's covenant sanctifies the natural bonds between parent and child so that the "natural" care the parent gives to the child becomes means of grace to him. God extends favor to David precisely in and through the favor shown by his

---

5. See Geoffrey Bromiley, *Children of the Promise: The Case For Baptizing Infants* (Grand Rapids: Eerdmans, 1998), 71–72. It might be asked: if this is true, why, then, in modern evangelicalism, do so many of our covenant children grow up and have a "conversion experience" at a later point in life? Certainly part of the reason so many of our children cannot relate directly to David's words is because we have *trained them* (that is, *conditioned them*) to seek after and interpret their experiences of God's grace through a different paradigm. We program them to think of themselves as unbelievers until they have the expected experience. We do not think they are (or can be) Christians until they get older.

The problem is not that the children lack faith, but that the adults do! They refuse to take the covenant promises about children seriously. They ignore the significance of infant baptism. I am not necessarily saying these conversions are "trumped up" by parental and ecclesial expectations, but I do think those expectations bear a lot of weight in shaping their Spiritual experiences.

If we applied the Davidic paradigm to our children (reckoning them as believers and treating them accordingly from infancy onward), we might be surprised at how their experiences would turn out quite differently (and considerably more in line with Psalm 22:8–9!). It is certainly possible for a child in a Christian home to have the gospel so clouded and obscured by false teaching, lack of loving discipline, a weak relationship with the local church, and so forth, that faith either stagnates or dies in youth, only to be revived at a later age. However, this kind of thing should never be the norm. Ordinarily, children in Christian homes should grow up Christian. I know that as I have reflected back on my own experience growing up as a covenant child, I have had to learn continually to re-narrate my past in light of a deeper understanding of God's Word, pushing the time of my "conversion experience" back from college, to high school, to elementary school, and finally to infancy. Hopefully, my own children will not have to do such re-narration, and "Davidspeak" will come naturally to them when they tell the story of God's gracious work in their lives.

parents. In a faithful home even a routine motherly task like nursing is not *merely* nursing, but a way in which the Spirit is communicated from God though the parent to the child (Jn. 7:38). In some mysterious way, nursing feeds not only David's body, but his faith. God's covenant promise and the work of the Spirit consecrate the organic bonds in the family so that parental care becomes a means of divine care. God gives Himself to the child through the labors and efforts of the parents. He blends His love in with their love.

## Psalm 71
Of course, Psalm 22 is not the only reference to paedofaith in the Psalter. We find something similar in Psalm 71:5–6. Here, the psalmist once again describes himself as having a trusting, personal relationship with God from his earliest days. God was the trust of his youth and continued to be the object of his praise as an adult. So here, for the child of the covenant, as in Psalm 22, the beginning of Spiritual life is coordinated with the beginning of physical life. When a sperm and egg unite in a covenant womb, the embryo already has a promise from God and an inescapable relationship with God.[6] This reiterates what we have already seen: God is a God to our children from the moment of conception, and being their God includes giving them a nascent faith. Christian embryos have embryonic faith.

---

6. This relationship is not a matter of *nature* but of *grace*. It is due to God's Spirit, not DNA. It is a matter of covenantal inheritance, not genetic inheritance. As soon as the new life is formed, that embryonic person is under the provisions of God's covenant promises. (This is why covenant promises would also apply to adopted children.)

Obviously, non-covenantal infants have a relationship with God from their earliest days as well, but it is a broken relationship. They are in Adam; Christ has made no explicit biblical promise to translate them out of the old humanity and into the new. There is no hard biblical evidence that they have the same favorable Godward orientation that covenant children have. In fact, there is a great deal of evidence to the contrary. They are related to God as covenant-breakers unless and until they repent. God may be mysteriously merciful to them if they die in infancy, but since Scripture is basically silent on this point, there's not much we can say. We can hope for un-covenanted mercies through the blood of Christ in such cases, but if God leaves these children to perish in their sin, He is fully just.

Specifically in 71:5, the psalmist speaks of having hope in God from his earliest days. Apparently, there was never a time in his life when he lived without this hope. In verse six he speaks of God's special care for him from birth. God brought him out of the womb safely, and it is this past track record of divine faithfulness that serves to bolster the psalmist's mature confidence that God will now deliver him from the wicked men who seek his harm and ruin (71:4). Because God has sheltered him with favor and care from his earliest days, He will continue to do so on into old age (71:9). From cradle to death bed, the Lord will be faithful to the covenant. This is the psalmist's assurance in a distressing time.

If we take the framework of the psalmist seriously, the covenant child would never need to pose the question, "What must I do to be saved?" That question would never even occur to the child. Salvation has belonged to him from the beginning because of God's covenant promise (71:6). He does not need a conversion experience when he reaches a mythical age of accountability. Instead, he simply needs to continue maturing and growing in the trust of his youth (71:5). Indeed, the psalmist pledges himself to just this kind of faith-filled perseverance later on in his prayer (71:14–18).

Certainly this paradigm of covenant nurture does not preclude the possibility of passing through various "crisis points" as the child matures. It does not mean the child's growth will be a straight upward climb. In Psalm 71 we find David facing challenges to his faith, but he does not allow the crisis to subvert his certainty that God has been with him the whole course of his life. As God brings him through the trial, he enters a new phase of maturity, but he will not confuse this with initial conversion. Infant faith does not negate the need for the child's growth; rather, it gives us a basis for expecting instruction, discipline, and nurture to be effective in the life of the child. Parents especially should take note of the way David interprets his experience. This should be our controlling paradigm in regard to our own children.[7]

---

7. Again, this helps us understand what is going on when kids today from faithful evangelical homes grow up and have what are often deemed "conversion" experiences. Evangelical culture does not consider infant faith a possibility, much less a probability, and so, practically speaking, children of Christian parents are regarded as any other category of unbelievers. We do not regard chil-

## Psalm 139

Another important psalm is 139. Psalm 139:14–15 has been pressed into generic usage because of contemporary debates over abortion, but these verses have a very specific, covenantal focus. Jack Collins, professor of Old Testament at Covenant Theological Seminary, suggests the following as the best translation of 139:14: "I praise you for the fact that I have been awesomely distinguished [as a member of your covenant people]; your works are wonderful, and my soul knows it well." Without repeating Collins' fine linguistic work on the passage, we should note the nu-

---

dren as part of God's believing family, so they do not regard themselves in this way either. However, these same children naturally desire to live up to parental expectations. We *insist* that that they have a decisive and dateable transition point, and they do so. However, in light of the above data, it is actually likely that such experiences are not about conversion per se except in the more general sense that the whole Christian life is one of continued deeper and deeper conversion from sin and unbelief to repentance and faith (e.g., Lk. 22:32). Think about David—he grew up trusting in God, but at several junctures in his life (as we know from numerous psalms!) he was "re-converted" and renewed as he passed through crisis situations. The same happens to all of us, including our children. Thus, we shouldn't discount their new experiences of God's grace as they hit puberty, go off to college, start families of their own, or face illnesses. These are experiences through which God brings true change, real spurts of Spiritual growth. We should be thankful for them.

But these "awakenings" or "mini-conversions," however powerful, should not be confused with initial conversion, as though the child was not a believer in any sense until he walked an aisle in elementary school, went off to a summer camp in high school, or got involved in a campus ministry in college. These experiences should be interpreted against the backdrop of texts like Psalm 22:9–10 and 71:5–6. The experiences are not necessarily problematic; the issue is our flawed understanding of them. Experience should be analyzed in light of Scripture, not nineteenth-century revivalist theology.

Many covenant children grow up and come to despise, or at least discount, the Christian nurture they were given in their youth. Because they were young, expressions of faith and piety were regarded as programmed and insincere. Likewise, they do not value the baptism they received in infancy. In this way, skepticism about the Spiritual experiences of children is perpetuated.

In addition, they may all too easily fall into a "once saved always saved" doctrine in which a one-time crisis conversion experience is said to secure salvation even apart from a subsequent life of obedience. This contrasts with the biblical teaching of the perseverance of the elect. All this fosters an unhealthy view of the means of grace and a hankering after the spectacular rather than an appreciation for God's more ordinary ways of working. We will take up this subject of covenant nurture in the final chapter.

ance of the verb "to be distinguished" in this context. Collins points out that each time this verb is used in the Old Testament (Ex. 9:4; 11:7; 33:16), "the distinction is one in which the covenant member is set apart for God's gracious attention." Thus, in Psalm 139:14, the psalmist is expressing awe, not simply over God's creative work in forming him in his mother's womb (as many translations imply); rather, he is praising God for having set him apart as a participant in His covenant of salvation. "In context this is praise that one's experience of God's covenantal blessings extends back to the very beginning of one's existence," as Collins puts it. This is not a generic declaration applicable to all *in utero* children; it is a special proclamation of God's care and favor for those children who belong to His covenant. These children are "awesomely distinguished" from children conceived outside the pale of the covenant community (cf. 1 Cor. 7:14).

Collins demonstrates persuasively that this translation and interpretation fit well with the rest of the psalm. In particular, the psalm focuses on the intimate knowledge God has of His people (139:1–6, 23–24). There is no place the psalmist can go that would take him outside the realm of God's care (139:7–12). Even in the womb, even before his own mother knew him, God knew the psalmist and loved him (139:13–18). In Psalm 139:19–22, then, the psalmist declares his loyalty to God in response to God's merciful provision. Finally, Collins says,

> verses twenty-three and twenty-four invite God to continue His examination all the length of the author's life, because the purging of his inner life from all impurity is the key to his remaining in the way to eternal blessedness.

The psalmist *entered* this way even in the womb; now he *continues* in that way by growing and maturing in his faith. Once again, we see that the covenant relationship extends from conception to expiration. This psalm contemplates the entire life of the covenant member, showing how his whole existence has been enveloped by God's mercy. The story runs from faith to ever-increasing faithfulness; from baby faith to ripened, mature faith.

Collins then echoes my earlier point about Psalm 22:9–10: it will not do to say that this is an experience unique to David. It has normative force, so we are warranted in applying it to covenant children as a class. All such children are conceived and grow up within the sphere of covenanted mercies.

> Is this simply a record of the personal experience of the author? No: whatever its origin, it is now in the Psalter, which means that its primary function is to provide fitting words for God's covenant people to use in their public corporate worship. The redemptive-historical setting of this psalm is an era in which virtually all the pious members of the covenant people were raised in what we would call believing covenant homes; and this psalm is equipping them to trace their experience of God's intimate love and care right back to the time they were embryos.
>
> The people sing that their relationship with God dates from their time in the womb. Indeed God's care for the children of His covenant people is inherent in the covenant itself (Gen. 17:7; 18:19; Ex. 34:7, "who keeps loving-kindness for thousands [of generations]"), so it is hardly surprising that it would figure in the worship of the covenant people.

Collins then adds a point of clarification:

> This means the "I" of the psalm is not "everyman" as such, but "every believing member of the covenant people" (and in context these were raised in covenant homes). Of course the Old Testament agrees with the New Testament in insisting that mere *external* membership in the covenant people is not sufficient: there must be the inner reality of faith, love, and loyalty toward God (without which external membership incurs a more severe judgment).[8]

---

8. All quotations are from C. John Collins, "Psalm 139:14: 'Fearfully and Wonderfully Made'?" *Presbyterion: Covenant Seminary Review*, 25/2 (Fall 1999), 115–20. In this last quotation, I am not totally comfortable with Collins' internal/external dualism. There no such thing as membership in the people of God that is merely external (e.g., sociological, with no Spiritual implications). That view, however prevalent, fails to reckon with the fact that the visible church is the kingdom of Christ, the house and family of God (WCF 25.2). Nevertheless, Collins' intended point—that church membership is not an automatic guarantee of salvation apart from faith—is entirely appropriate.

Psalm 139 does not contain an explicit reference to the psalmist's paedofaith the way Psalm 22 and Psalm 71 do. However, it is not at all difficult to see the connection between the way David describes his *in utero* experience of grace here with the way it is described elsewhere. Even in the womb the relationship between David and his God is so intimate that it must have been one of mutual faithfulness. It is not simply that God knew (loved) David, but that David knew (loved) God. Surely such knowing and loving on David's part included faith. The covenant distinction that set David apart even in the womb strongly suggests the presence of embryonic trust. How could he be sanctified apart from the work of Spirit? And what prevents the Spirit from working—in even the youngest and most immature—a relationship of trust toward God?[9]

---

9. If we deny this point, we are denying that the new humanity is co-extensive with the old humanity. We would be, in principle, sealing off a sector of God's creation from Christ's redeeming work. A segment of humanity would be placed outside the reach of salvation. If God's plan of redemption involves reclaiming His fallen creation from the curse (cf. Rom. 8:17ff), then humans of every age, station, and ethnicity must be open to receiving salvation, including embryos. Peter Leithart explains this point in terms of the rationale for infant baptism. "Adam sinned, and instead of life and glory, humanity plunged into death and shame. Yet, God did not give up on His original plan to form a human race that would share in His glory and life. He called Abraham to be the father of this race, and Israel became the new humanity. Israel was not merely a "religious" group among other religious groups. Israel was the nation called to live in the presence of the Creator, in communion with the Creator, as all humanity was called to live. Yahweh intended for Israel to be the seed of a new human race. To show that Israel was a new human race and not merely a club for religious people, the infants of Israel, the males, were formally incorporated into Israel. Israel included all sorts and conditions of men—infants, toddlers, teenagers, adults, the elderly—because the human race included all sorts and conditions of men. And Israel was the human race renewed.

"Like Adam, Israel failed to be what the Creator called her to be. And yet God the Creator did not give up on His plan to form a human race that would share in His glory and life. What Israel could not do, weak as she was in the flesh, God did. God sent His Son to become Israel, to do what Israel had not done, to recapitulate the life and history of Israel but to reverse it by living the history of Israel righteously. God's intention in Jesus was His original intention with Adam, to form a new Israel, the truly new human race, through and in the Son of God. And, like Israel, this new Israel includes all sorts and conditions of men—infants, toddlers, teenagers, adults, the elderly—because it is the human

Psalm 139:15 is also interesting in regard to the question of paedofaith. The psalmist speaks of God having "woven" him together in his mother's womb. The verb used here does more than merely indicate that each new conception and gestation is a work of God through created means and processes. This verb is used elsewhere in the Old Testament to describe the making of the veils and curtains that hung in the tabernacle (Ex. 26:36). The covenant infant is woven together, like fine fabric, for holy purposes. The child is already a sacred person (cf. 1 Cor. 7:14), a kind of mini-temple in which God dwells by His Spirit (cf. 1 Cor. 6:19). Obviously the child will enter a greater degree of holiness at circumcision/baptism, and will need to grow up into his covenantal status by professing faith and walking in obedience in the years to come. His paedofaith must grow into mature, more fully-actualized adult faith. But the covenant child's starting point should be clear: he belongs to the Lord; he is God's special workmanship; he is a temple of the Holy Spirit; he is a member of the believing covenant people. David's language, including its intertextual resonances, makes no sense apart from the presupposition of paedofaith.

## Psalm 8

Psalm 8 is also relevant to our discussion of paedofaith. Here we are dealing with children outside the womb, and David, as the author, regards even nursing babes as warriors in the Lord's army (8:2). Their praise is heard by God and is effective in Israel's holy war. Their inarticulate babblings are accepted by God as beautiful worship and powerful praise.

---

race renewed. The Church, marked out by the water-boundary of baptism, is, theoretically if not actually, coextensive with the human race.

"You see, if you refuse to baptize infants, then you are saying that God's plans have changed. Once upon a time, God intended to form a new human race that would share His life and glory. But that plan failed, so He has now decided to gather together adults who will share in that life and glory.

"Infant baptism, then, is not some extraneous and odd practice of the Church. It is bound up with the whole plan and purpose of God. In baptism, we are retelling the story of the human race, and of God's redemption, which is a fulfillment of creation." From Leithart's website, http://www.leithart.com/archives/001274_print.php. The biblical doctrine of paedofaith is further evidence that the new humanity includes families and nations, not just isolated, matured individuals. (Families and nations include infants, after all!) Paedofaith is just one aspect of a "new humanity" ecclesiology.

Assuming David means what he says, we have to ask: How could these young children praise God without faith? How could they silence the foe and avenger without trusting the Lord? While it may be difficult to explain how nursing babes could be believers, it seems even more difficult to explain how these same children could be so Spiritually active and effective *without* faith! Denying the "problem" of infant faith only creates a larger problem.

This psalm envisions God using even the most helpless and the weakest to bring down His enemies.[10] David mentions babes and nursing infants—obviously a reference to very young children, at least some of whom would not have fully developed speech or intellectual abilities. The spectrum covered by these terms for children ranges from birth to toddler. These two categories are paired up with "the enemy and the avenger." The enemy and the avenger may appear strong, but the Lord uses the verbal, babbling praise of these young covenant children to silence their accusations. God works through the lowliest of the low to bring in His victorious kingdom.

By setting covenant infants in the context of holy war, this psalm also helps us understand the task of Christian parenting. As parents, we must (by faith) view our children as warriors in the Lord's army. They are on active duty even in their infancy, but we must continue to train them to obey their Commander-in-Chief more fully as they mature. They will learn more and more how to wield their weapons, use their defensive armor, and follow out the Captain's battle strategy. But this passage indicates they are conscripted by the Lord from their earliest days; the Lord does not need to wait for them to develop intellectually and physically because He is the one who fights through them. Indeed, young children are some of the best soldiers in the Lord's army precisely because His strength is manifested in their weakness (cf. 2 Cor. 12:9). This does not mean their immaturity remains ideal; they must grow up over time, attaining to maturity in Christ. However, it does mean that even before they

---

10. Obviously, this psalm is ultimately fulfilled in Christ himself. He becomes the nursing babe who defeats the enemies of God through the worship of His Father.

grow they are able to fight. God has already stationed them on the battle-field.

It simply will not do to say that infants here *symbolize* weak adult human beings, as though the babes and infants in Psalm 8:2 only served as metaphors. Such a reading robs the psalm of its force. Besides, it crashes into the New Testament usage of this passage. Matthew 21:12–17 records Jesus' temple cleansing, amidst the cheers of children, portraying the event as a prophetic fulfillment of Psalm 8:2 (among other Old Testament prophesies). In this recasting of Psalm 8:2 the chief priests and scribes are the "enemy and the avenger," whose objections to Jesus are silenced by the praising chorus of children (Mt. 21:15–16). Jesus stops up the mouths of His accusers by pointing to the children who have been crying out, "Hosanna to the Son of David!" These children have identified Jesus as Messiah, the One who brings the Lord's salvation. The Jewish religious leaders are offended by the cry of the children, but Jesus accepts their praise. The arrogant become indignant over the cries of the children, but Jesus is delighted by them. The children manifest a greater degree of Spiritual perception than the priests and scribes, a typical example of a gospel reversal. We are forced to ask: Is our attitude toward children more like Jesus or His enemies? Do we treat their claims to love God as mere lip service or as the fruit of the Spirit's work in them? Are we skeptical of the praises, professions, and experiences of small covenant children? Or do we believe that through such humble means, God has "perfected praise" (Mt. 21:16)?

We also see here another important aspect of training covenant children. The shouts of these children in the temple (Mt. 21:15) echo the praises of the whole multitude during the triumphal entry (Mt. 21:9). The children were part of that multitude, no doubt, and now they are continuing that same form of worship on their own in the temple. This reveals the value of liturgy for children: they can easily memorize repeated prayer forms and make them their own.[11] Jesus does not reject their praises be-

---

11. Anyone who has read stories to children or played games with them knows firsthand how much they are creatures of habit. G. K. Chesterton rightfully identified love for ritual (and thus liturgy) as a sign of youthful vitality. See his *Orthodoxy* (New York: Doubleday Books, 1990 reprint), 60–61. The symbols and rituals of historic liturgy provide children with a way to "say more than they

cause they were "scripted"—because they used the same language as their elders, rather than their own spontaneous words. Parents should make liturgical routines a part of life for their children so that their children grow up with the great creeds—the Lord's Prayer, the *Doxology*, the *Gloria Patri*, the *Te Deum*, and so on—flowing in their blood. Just as these children had been given the words to use in their praise of God, so we should fill our children's mouths with the language of biblical and traditional worship forms as well. Liturgical patterns of worship are the best way to help our

---

know." They are embodying their faith in a way that leaves room for (and even encourages) growth and development. They are (perhaps subconsciously) learning to identify themselves with the community of faith and its traditions. A wellcrafted liturgy evokes a sense of mystery, awakens the imagination, and gives a sense of connection to something bigger than the individual self. Eastern Orthodox theologian Alexander Schmemann, in a document available at http://www.schmemann .org/byhim/childrenandchurch.html, captures well the way in which liturgy appeals to children. "As a general rule, children like attending Church, and this instinctive attraction to and interest in Church services is the foundation on which we must build our religious education. When parents worry that children will get tired because services are long and are sorry for them, they usually subconsciously express their concern not for their children but for themselves. Children penetrate more easily than do adults into the world of ritual, of liturgical symbolism. They feel and appreciate the atmosphere of our church services. The experience of Holiness, the sense of encounter with Someone Who is beyond daily life, that *mysterium tremendum* that is at the root of all religion and is the core of our services is more accessible to our children than it is to us. 'Except ye become as little children,' these words apply to the receptivity, the open-mindedness, the naturalness, which we lose when we grow out of childhood. How many men have devoted their lives to the service of God and consecrated themselves to the church because from childhood they have kept their love for the house of worship and the joy of liturgical experience! Therefore, the first duty of parents and educators is to 'suffer little children and forbid them not' (Mt. 19:14) to attend church. It is in church before every place else that children must hear the word of God. In a classroom the word is difficult to understand, it remains abstract, but in church it is in its own element. In childhood we have the capacity to understand, not intellectually, but with our whole being, that there is no greater joy on earth than to be in Church, to participate in Church services, to breathe the fragrance of the Kingdom of Heaven, which is 'the joy and peace of the Holy Spirit.' " Of course, parents who (rightly) seek to include their children in the Church's worshipping assemblies should remember that the point is not merely to have the children in the room with us, but to train them in the skills of authentic worship (e.g., to learn to sing, to say the scripted responses, to say the Creed and the Lord's Prayer, etc.), as Schmemann suggests.

children offer "perfect praise." These forms will give their youthful faith something solid to feed upon for the rest of their lives.[12]

Psalm 8:2, especially as it is used in Matthew 21, gives us an example of paedofaith in action. Here we have small children young enough to still be nursing, yet the feeble praise they offer is not only accepted by God, it is used by Him to topple the enemies of His kingdom. It may be praise offered in a form of words given to them in the liturgy, but it is regarded as sincere nonetheless. Plus, in the light of the New Testament appropriation of this psalm, we can say these small children are able to recognize Jesus and know Him (in some form or fashion) as the Davidic King and Savior. They know the One they are worshipping by faith; by faith their praises are made acceptable.

This may not be paedofaith in the strictest sense (since at least some of the children here are a bit older), but it is fully compatible with the more explicit references to paedofaith seen elsewhere in the Psalter earlier in our survey. God holds small covenant children in high regard. He encourages and receives their praise. This hospitable, welcoming attitude toward covenant children on the part of God is a model for us.

## Psalms 127 and 128

The final pieces of evidence we will consider are derived from Psalms 127 and 128. Here, children given to covenant-keeping parents are called "a heritage from the Lord" and a "reward" (127:3). In other words, one way God blesses the godly is with godly offspring. These

---

12. Liturgy is also of great pastoral use for the elderly. Indeed, liturgical worship is perhaps the best form of cradle-to-grave pastoral care churches can give their people. In the liturgy, we learn the faith as nursing babes as we are taught the language of orthodoxy in set, ritualized forms (confessions, catechisms, creeds, hymns, psalms, prayers, etc.). By faith, these fixed patterns shape our minds and hearts and become woven in the very fabric of our being. They strengthen the fibers of community life and enable us to make orthodox devotion the very environment we inhabit. As life's end draws near, decades of liturgical worship stockpiled in our memory enable us to die with the faith still on our lips. For a wonderful, highly anecdotal look at liturgy's enduring value in the life of the Christian, see Robert Zagore's article, "Serving Us Until Our Dying Breath," available at http://mypage.direct.ca/j/jlove/tchissues/tch0398.htm. For a more sweeping defense of liturgy, see Jeffery Meyers' *The Lord's Service: The Grace of Covenant Renewal Worship* (Moscow, ID: Canon Press, 2003).

children come from God; He is the builder of the house of the faithful (cf. 127:1). The godly man does not need to stay up late worrying about how to guard his children or scheming ways to provide for his house; instead, he should sleep in peace, trusting the Lord's sure provision and protection (127:1–2). Covenant children are a gift, not a burden, to the man who lives by faith in the Lord and in godly fear. Indeed, the great hope of the righteous is to see the faith passed on from one generation to the next, on into the future (128:6). Covenant succession is one of the ultimate blessings of the covenant. It is considered normative.

The godly man finds in his own children a reward from the Lord, but what kind of reward would God be giving if these children did not come with a covenant promise that included their faith? The children given to the godly are like arrows in the quiver of the warrior (127:4–5). They are on the faithful side of the covenantal antithesis. The godly man does not have children in order to fill Satan's forces or populate hell, but in order to reclaim the earth for the kingdom of God as warriors in the great cosmic battle of history.

Here, as in Psalm 8, the covenantal nature of the child and the task of Christian parenting are seen to mesh together fully. The children God gives are an inheritance and a reward, meaning they are His special gift and blessing. Even in the womb, before they can do anything useful for God or humanity, they are regarded as great treasures. Again, martial imagery is used: they are warriors contending with the enemy in the city gate. They are weapons with which to fight the wicked. As in Psalm 8, covenant children are already regarded as participants in the great holy war of history. Covenant children are arrows aimed at the heart of the enemy. If parents shoot them with faith-homed accuracy, they will hit the target and strike a blow for the cause of the gospel.[13]

Psalm 128 adds horticultural imagery to this picture. Covenant children are like olive plants gathered around the table. This makes parents gardeners. Parents are not given weeds for children who must then be converted into wholesome plants. Rather, they are given the best possible plants to work with. They are to care for and nurture these

---

13. Unlike Psalm 8, nothing is said here of the age of the children in view. But in light of Psalm 8, there is no reason to limit the reference to grown children.

plants in the greenhouses of home and church until the children are mature, fruit-bearing trees. The family culture is to incubate these precious plants in a context of holy joy and fellowship.

Why are the children of the God-fearing man called olive plants? Olive plants were the holiest of all vegetation in the old covenant symbolic system.[14] The olive tree itself was a regular image of the covenant people (Rom. 11:16–24) and the temple of God, especially the Holy of Holies (Zech. 4; Rev. 11:4).[15] The oil flowing through the plant was a symbol of the Holy Spirit.[16] Jesus' ministry climaxed in an Olivet environment.[17] In God's view our children are not weeds, but the holiest plants in the garden. They belong to the covenant community, the royal priesthood, the new temple, and are filled with the oil of the Spirit.

---

14. Some Jewish traditions regarded the Tree of Life in Eden as an olive tree. The olive branch is a symbol of peace and new creation (Gen. 8:11). Olives had a wide variety of uses in Israelite culture, including liturgical usage. They were among the most highly valued plants in the ancient orient. Interestingly, in order to reach their full potential, olives must be pruned regularly. References to olives abound throughout the Scriptures as well as in Christian art and poetry.

15. Symbolically, the temple was an olive grove (cf. Ps. 52:8). The Holy of Holies was guarded by olive trees (cf. 1 Ki. 6:23–24), symbolic of priests.

16. Harvested olive oil was used in anointing which symbolized the outpouring of the Spirit on a person or object (Ex. 30:22–33). The Spirit's association with olive oil also traces back to Genesis 8:11 when the dove carried an olive branch back to Noah. Olive oil was used in the offerings of the Levitical sacrificial system as well.

17. Jesus' ministry peaked on the Mount of Olives, a grove of olive trees. From this location, an ad hoc "Holy of Holies," He pronounced final judgment on the temple in Jerusalem (cf. Mt. 24; Ezek. 10–11). Olives were in the Garden of Gethsemane (the olive press; cf. Mt. 26:30) as well, and it is likely that Jesus was crucified on an olive tree (cf. Acts 5:30; 10:39; 13:29; etc.) since Golgotha was located on the Mount of Olives (cf. Zech. 14:4). Symbolically this placed Jesus in the Holy of Holies as He completed His earthly ministry, since the innermost sanctuary was symbolically an olive grove (cf. 1 Ki. 6:23–24). In the resurrection, Mary Magdalene confused Jesus with the olive-gardener, but of course, in a very real sense, she was exactly right: as a new Adam, in the olive garden, He will tend to the olive tree of His people, the new covenant temple (cf. Jn. 19:41; 20:15; see also Rom. 11:16ff). Finally, Jesus ascended to heaven from the Mount of Olives (Acts 1:12). Olive trees are linked with heavenly access. All this should factor into what it means to regard our children as olive plants gathered around the familial "holy of holies," the kitchen table.

Note that these plants are gathered around the *table* (128:3). This is a family that eats meals together. It is not a family in which each member centers life on something that takes him or her outside of the home at any and every possible moment. It is an environment of shared fellowship and shared meals and shared lives. It is a family that embraces and embodies the covenant relations they share. It is a family in which the slogan is (as Thomas Howard, and now Douglas Wilson, have put it), "My life for yours."[18] The wife/mother is held in especially high esteem as the heart of the house (128:3). She is a fruitful vine, and her fruits certainly include their children. While it is *his* house, she is the primary shaper of the family culture, the heartbeat of its life and the source of its joy. This is the meaning of the vine image (obviously pointing to wine, the fruit of the vine, which makes the hearts of men glad; cf. Ps. 104:15; Song of Songs 1:2, 4; 4:10; 7:9, etc.).

The parental task, then, in light of Psalms 127 and 128, is to receive our children as gifts from the Lord, giving thanks for them and getting to work with them. The vocation of the Christian parent is to rejoice in his heritage (127:3; 128:2–3) and to make sure he does not squander his inheritance by failing to nurture his children unto maturity. He is to continually equip and strengthen his children for battle, so they will not be ashamed when they confront their enemies face-to-face in the city gate. Parents should make these young arrows ever sharper and straighter, aiming them more and more accurately at the enemies of God. They should fertilize and nurture the holy olive plants in the garden of their homes until they grow up to maturity, bearing fruit for the Lord.

There is not a hint in these texts that our children need to undergo a conscious conversion experience before they can be regarded as arrows or olives. Indeed, the lack of any such reference indicates our children should be regarded as belonging to the Lord by faith from infancy onward. God does not reward us with unclean, unbelieving children; He gives us an inheritance and reward of children who relate to Him in a posture of trust from the very outset of their lives. Because covenant

---

18. See Thomas Howard, *Splendor in the Ordinary* (Manchester, NH: Sophia Institute Press, 2000), and Douglas Wilson, *My Life for Yours* (Moscow, ID: Canon Press, 2004). Both of these books are excellent, highly practical studies of family culture.

children are given Spirit-wrought faith, they are a blessing and not a curse to us.

## Conclusion

What conclusions can we draw from the Psalter as a whole? Several major points stand out. Even though the Psalter is the encyclopedia of Christian experience, it *nowhere* catalogs a covenant child having a conversion experience. It *does* record explicit and implicit cases of paedofaith. David has many momentous, wrenching experiences, but a revivalist-style conversion experience is not among them. The Psalter treats infant trust not as a sporadic, occasional, or unpredictable reality, but as the norm in covenant children. God gives us believing children to work with and nurture. In this way, covenant children are a blessing and a reward from the Lord. As we help them grow to mature faith, we fulfill the purpose of the cross-generational covenant promises. The psalmist has many remarkably deep, vivid, datable, and narratable experiences of God's grace, but he still maintains he was a believer from infancy; he trusted in God and knew Him from the very beginning of life. In this way, the Psalter norms Christian experience for the child growing up in a Christian environment. The experience of the psalmist should be the experience of our offspring. Our children belong to Christian homes and, like David, should learn to regard themselves as believers from infancy onward, not necessarily on the basis of experience, but as a corollary of the covenant promises.

Further, covenant children should be nurtured in the faith all along the way from infancy forward to young adulthood. They should learn to view their prior experiences of God's grace (such as God's care for them in the womb and at birth) as a sign of His continued commitment to them into the future. They should be trained in liturgical worship forms so they can silence God's enemies through prayer and praise. They should be regarded as fellow soldiers in the Lord's army, graciously conscripted by their participation in the covenant promises and enlisted through the sacrament of initiation (circumcision/baptism). They are olive plants, meaning they are holy guardians in God's sanctuary, filled with the oil of anointing, namely, the Spirit of peace and re-creation. They are God's reward and inheritance through which He builds up the houses of the faithful.

We should not be skeptical of their Spiritual experiences and their feeble worship; instead, we should expect them to live in an environment wholly conditioned by God's grace and truth. They are awesomely distinguished even from the womb as God weaves them together into a holy dwelling place for His Son and Spirit; they are sharp arrows aimed at the hearts of God's enemies; they are a heritage from the Lord and a great reward to the faithful; they are model soldiers and worshippers in the Lord's liturgical army. This is the Psalter's theology of covenant children.

two

## *paedofaith in the gospels*

God says He will be a God to us and to our children. To be our God
means to be our Savior and Redeemer. It means that God's gospel is our
possession. It means all His promises are our special treasure and all
His power is put in the service of our salvation. To be our God and our
children's God means He is our heavenly Father, and we are members
of His family. In other words, the covenant promises of the Old Testament indicate that God saves our children. The means through which
He does this is by giving them faith. Moreover, the old covenant record
indicates this is true from the moment our children are brought into
existence in the wombs of their mothers. So far from overturning this
covenantal teaching, we find it reinforced and intensified in the new
covenant Scriptures, only here, the declarations are even greater. In the
new eon, covenant children are not merely included in the Israel of
God; they are enfolded into the eschatological kingdom of heaven.

We have already hinted that infant faith is not just an Old Testament phenomenon, but now we need to look at New Testament data

more closely. We will not attempt a comprehensive overview, but will focus our attention on a few critical texts in the gospels. Here we will find abundant confirmation and enrichment of the picture of covenant children already sketched in the previous chapter.

### Jesus and John the Baptist

Let us begin with the example of John the Baptist. While his case is a bit unique, it is still representative. His role in redemptive history is to symbolize the old covenant as the way is made ready for the coming of Christ and the kingdom of God (Mt. 11:11–12). In the womb of his mother, Elizabeth, John leaped for joy when brought into the presence of his Lord and Savior, who was also *in utero* at the time (Lk. 1:41). John was a new David, already relating to God from before birth. He was holy, sanctified, and faithful. He saluted his Master and Savior when he drew near to Him.

Like Psalms 22 and 71, this is irrefutable proof that infants are capable of Spiritual relationships. How could John have perceived the presence of Jesus apart from faith and the work of the Spirit? Somehow John was able to interact personally with Jesus, womb to womb. He was in relationship with Jesus, even at that early stage of life. Like David in the Psalter, he is already hoping in and interfacing with the Lord even before birth.[1]

---

1. Obviously, there is much here that is mysterious. Usually relationships are formed and maintained through means such as signs and rituals. In this case, the means involved would be rather minimal. But, however mysterious paedo-relationships may be, they are clearly a part of God's world. Infants are not sub-personal. They are capable of interacting with others at their own level and in their own way. To deny that infants can have faith is to deny they can have in-terpersonal relationships; to deny they can have relationships is to deny they are persons; to deny they are persons is to open the door to anti-Christian practices such as abortion. Insofar as the "pro-life" viewpoint hinges on establishing the personhood of the child in the womb, paedofaith bolsters the anti-abortion ar-gument, while the denial of paedofaith weakens it. If embryos are persons, they can have faith. Paedofaith is no more absurd than the pro-life position. Some theologians may scoff at the idea of embryonic faith, but we should remember that many liberals today scoff at the idea that embryos are persons in any sense whatsoever. Whereas Scripture sees a new person being formed (Ps. 139:14–15), most secular non-Christians just see a clump of cells. But if the zygote actually bears the image of God from conception onward and is en-souled (that is, it is a

## Matthew 18:1–14

Later in the gospel accounts we find this dynamic of infant faith greatly expanded upon by Jesus. The entire pericope of Matthew 18:1–14 deserves careful study. This is perhaps the most comprehensive theology of covenant children in the entire Bible. In this passage, Jesus ties together virtually every thread of theology related to covenant children.

In context, the disciples have been arguing about their respective ranks in the kingdom of God (cf. Mk. 9:33–37). Jesus called a child to Himself in order to give them a paradoxical definition of greatness in the kingdom—it is characterized by child-like trust and humility, rather than worldly power and fame (18:2–4). Jesus makes children the paradigmatic members of His kingdom. He does not say little children have to *grow up* and become like adults (complete with mature, articulated faith) in order to enter the kingdom; instead, adults must become like children.

Here we can state an important principle: *all initial faith is paedofaith.* And we can add another closely related point: therefore, *all baptisms are paedobaptisms.* We all enter the kingdom as babies (cf. the new birth theme in John 3). Children, after all, know they are helpless and dependent on the resources of others. There is no pretension or posturing when it comes to children. Thus they reveal the pathway *into* the kingdom. They embody kingdom greatness in their self-abandoning trust and vulnerability. In absolute opposition to revivalism (as if He knew it would someday arise in the life of the church), Jesus does not say the little child has to be converted in order to enter the kingdom; instead, He says adults must convert into children to enter the kingdom (18:3). Somehow we have managed to reverse Jesus' demands for kingdom entrance. We demand adult-like conversions from children. We demand they convert into adults to enter the kingdom, but it is not so in the gospels. Jesus presupposed the child in His arms was converted; modern evangelicals tend to assume the opposite. The adults, not the child, are in need of conversion

body/soul creation), the possibility of paedofaith has to be seriously considered. See "When Does Personhood Begin?" by Bob Smietana available at http://www.christianitytoday.com/ct/2004/007/7.24.html. Also of interest is the debate over personhood and abortion available at http://www.religioustolerance .org/abo_when.htm.

in this narrative as Matthew presents it.[2]

It is important that Jesus called a little child to Himself as an object lesson in the context of the disciples raising questions about *greatness* (18:1; cf. 20:20ff; Mk. 9:30–37). Jesus used that child to rebuke their petty and self-centered aspirations. Jesus' definition of kingdom greatness is a direct affront to, and reversal of, the disciples' understanding of greatness. According to Jesus, in the economy of His kingdom, the way to greatness is through humility; the way up to glory is down in service; the way to maturity is found in child-like faith; the way to strength is through weakness. His kingdom turns their values upside down and inside out. He completely confounds their expectations—so much so they seemed to miss the point entirely (cf. Mt. 19:13). In Jesus' estimation, children are great because they are so vulnerable and humble.

The disciples are still operating on a worldly value scale which has little place for children. They still think the first will be first (cf. Mk. 9:35). They view children as a nuisance, a distraction, an interruption. Children are an unwanted reminder of human frailty and weakness, and get in the way of life's really important matters. They have not yet learned that only those who admit they are weak and helpless can be beneficiaries of Jesus' kingdom. They have not yet learned that Jesus values the very things they despise.

Jesus subverts the disciples' assumptions about personal worth by holding up a child as a model.[3] Jesus puts the child on the same level as the disciples. This would be preposterous, of course, if the child had no faith. Why exhort the disciples to follow the example of an unbeliever?

---

2. Given the way Jesus is making His point, we might say the younger the child is, the better illustration he is of this kind of kingdom-entering faith. The more the helplessness and neediness are obvious, the better, for it is precisely that helplessness that exalts and magnifies the sovereign and free grace of God.

3. Even more to the point, behind the words of Jesus here we have His own example. In the incarnation, the eternally begotten Son "became a child" and lived as a child in order to enter into His Father's kingdom. Jesus is the supreme model of child-like trust and humility. In becoming man—and a baby in a manger no less—the eternal Son reveals to us the ultimate act of self-negation. It is absolutely paradoxical as the eternal and all-powerful One subjects Himself to the limitations and helplessness of infanthood. For further thoughts, see Peter Leithart's "Baptism Meditation" available at http://www.leithart.com/archives/001081_print.php.

The child can only display the way into the kingdom if he possesses a humble, self-abandoning faith. It is this child-like trust that unlocks the door to the kingdom of heaven. Children and adults enter the kingdom in precisely the same way, but that entryway is more graphically displayed by children. Children are a blessing to parents (and the whole church), at least in part, because they provide a living illustration of the kind of faith all kingdom members must manifest. So far from being unbelievers, Jesus holds them up as exemplary models of kingdom-possessing faith.

By locating covenant children within the sphere of the kingdom, Jesus indicates that children are capable of receiving the benefits of His redemptive work. If our children are *in the kingdom* (Mt. 18:3–4) and *of the kingdom* (Mt. 19:14), Jesus is clearly regarding them as regenerate believers since the kingdom is seen and entered by faith (cf. Jn. 3). He treats them as "little Davids." He indicates that God is their God even in youth. He suggests that they have a trusting relationship with Him from their earliest days.

Insofar as the gifts of the kingdom can only be accepted by faith, Jesus' declaration that these children possess the kingdom of God emphatically assures us that they do in fact have faith. They must be able to exercise faith even though they cannot grasp the content of the preached Word. Their faith must be a matter of relational disposition, since it would generally lack propositional content, but it is faith nonetheless.

Receiving these children in Christ's name (Mt. 18:5) means receiving them as gifts of Christ and bearers of Christ's presence. It means we regard our children as belonging to Christ's body and bride and as being indwelt by His Spirit and covered by the atoning love of the cross. It also entails bringing them to those places where Christ has promised to be present to meet them.[4] It means receiving them in light of the promises

---

4. Charles Spurgeon objected to infant baptism by arguing that children were to be brought to Jesus, rather than to the font. But this is a false disjunction. Jesus makes Himself present precisely in the waters of baptism. The command to baptize includes a promise of His presence (Mt. 28:18–20). He offers Himself to us in baptism, to be received by faith (cf. Rom. 6:1ff; Gal. 3:27). We ought to bring our children into Christ's presence in every way we can (baptism, Eucharist, prayer, worship).

He has made about them and treating them as members of the covenant people. It certainly means baptizing them as a ritualized way of welcoming them into the kingdom and inviting them to Christ's table as a way of showing them hospitality and care within the kingdom. It means viewing them as Jesus would view them, as fellow heirs of the kingdom of God.

Jesus designates covenant children as special representatives of His presence (18:5; cf. Mk. 9:36).[5] The language used here is similar to language used elsewhere for His specially-commissioned servants; indeed, we may say covenant children are miniature quasi-apostles of Christ (cf. Mt. 18:5, Mk. 9:37, and Lk. 9:46–48 with Mt. 10:40–42). Christ sends "apostles" into Christian homes every time a baby is born. He visits the family in the person of the child. He sends the child in His name and as His emissary.

The point is clear: how you treat the youngest and most vulnerable members of the covenant family is how you treat Christ Himself. They are members of Christ's body, so what we do to and for them is done to and for Christ. How we handle these covenant children reveals either the pride or humility buried in our hearts; our posture toward children is the ultimate litmus test for whether or not we are willing to live sacrificially. We are to welcome covenant children into our lives as we would welcome Christ Himself or one of His apostles. Every child of the covenant is a christ-child (small "c") and an apostle (small "a").

---

5. Many older scholastic commentators argued that at this point in the text Jesus is using "little child" and "little ones" as a metaphor for adult disciples who possess a child-like trust and humility. On that reading, the scribes and Pharisees are the ones who cause disciples to stumble by turning them away from Jesus. As punishment, they would be cast into the sea of Roman legions in the Jewish War of 66–70 AD. (The sea is a frequent Old Testament image for Gentile political powers.) The strength of this reading is that it gives a seamless flow into a discussion of church discipline in 18:15ff.

Today, the balance of commentators has shifted toward those who view Jesus as talking about actual children in this whole pericope. Obviously, I see this interpretation as the superior reading, but there is no reason why the passage cannot be read at more than one level, both literally ("little ones" being covenant children) and metaphorically ("little ones" being adult disciples). We can easily slide back and forth between these levels because Jesus has set up an analogical relationship in 18:3. The warning in verses six through ten is clear: anyone who turns a disciple, young or old, away from the kingdom will receive the harshest of judgments. Beware of offenses!

But note the key point made here for purposes of this study: Jesus completely identifies Himself with the little children, which would be odd, to say the least, if little children were not capable of having faith or being personally connected to Him. Indeed, Jesus' words presuppose these children are in union with Him. They have faith *precisely because* they are united to the Faithful One; they share in His life of faithfulness. Jesus is regarding these children as little believers, united to Him by faith in a bond of covenanted love. It is unlawful for us to pry Jesus apart from those He regards as His own. To do so is to assault Jesus Himself; it is to seek to amputate members of His body. We must not separate what God has joined together, namely, Jesus and our children.

In Matthew 18:6, Jesus makes the presupposition of infant faith—implicit in verses two through five—explicit. He speaks of "the little ones who *believe* in Me." There is nothing in the passage to indicate that the little child Jesus was using as Exhibit A (18:2) was a unique, one-off specimen. Instead, that child was illustrative of the *entire category* of covenant children. That child represented an entire segment of believers, a group especially vulnerable to stumbling into apostasy, should older folks hinder them in their covenanted relationship to Jesus. Nothing in the passage indicates that only *some* covenant children belong to the kingdom or are included in Jesus' welcome. Indeed, the strong inclusivity of the text makes it hard to imagine that Jesus would have turned away *any* covenant child. I would not want to conclude from this that absolutely all covenant infants have faith (again, we'll take up this question later), but, as with Psalm 22, infant faith certainly appears to be the norm. Covenant children are small believers. They should be received as such. They are given to us walking with Jesus in faith; we dare not make them stumble.

The sin of the children in view in verse six is clearly apostasy. Adults are severely warned to do nothing that might cause their little ones to fall away from the faith. When adults sin in regard to their children, they put their children in a dangerous position. Parents especially are responsible for the impressions they make upon their children, for better or worse. Those who have responsibility for caring for covenant children (which is everyone in the church in some form or fashion!) should constantly encourage the growth of their faith, and do nothing that would cause them to turn away from Christ in unbelief.

Here we must stop and ask a very practical set of questions: What might cause these paedobelievers to apostatize? How can parents, in particular, trip up little ones who have been walking with Christ? We can think of several ways for parents to hinder and even destroy their children. Parents who set a bad example by overt sin and/or hypocrisy tempt their children to stumble. Children will almost always grow to mirror the private character of their parents. Life patterns are generally "caught" as much as "taught" and parents who fail to deal with their own sin will find those same sins magnified in the lives of their children. When parents sin against their children, they should be quick to confess, repent, and make amends. Otherwise, the child eventually picks up on a double standard.

Parents who refuse to consistently teach and discipline their children put a stumbling stone before them. They fail to inculcate the virtues and habits of Christian living in their children. By indulging their children, they fail to teach them that they will reap what they sow. Parental negligence is culpable.[6]

Similarly, parents who are too busy to pray with and for their children also set up obstacles. They end up parenting in their own strength rather than by faith. Whatever parental works of instruction and correction they do perform become nothing more than works of the flesh. Yet biblically, raising covenant children should be done in an environment saturated by humble, promise-based prayer because such prayer is the language of faith.

Covenant parents who treat their little children as no better than rank outsiders or pagans also drive their children away from Christ, as do those parents who hold their children up against perfectionistic

---

6. An example of a generation of parents who caused their children to stumble is recorded for us in Judges 2:10. While the parents remained faithful themselves, they allowed their children to fall away, because the parents were negligent in exterminating the idols from the land. This became the point of stumbling. All the work Joshua's generation put into conquering the land was wasted because these parents failed to train their children properly. This episode in Israel's story is all the more sad because it comes on the historical heels of Joshua's bold, exemplary declaration, "As for me and my house, we will serve the Lord" (Josh. 24:15).

standards and make impossible demands. Such parents do not receive their children as Christ's representatives (18:5), and in driving a wedge between their children and Christ, they put themselves and their children in danger. By excluding their children from the kingdom (for all practical purposes) they risk excluding themselves.

Parents who demand too much or too little can end up exasperating their children. Parents who are inconsistent in what they require or how they enforce their standards can frustrate and unnecessarily discourage their children. Parents who only deal with the externals of behavior, and ignore the issues of the heart, mislead and misdirect their children.

Jesus says those who are responsible for the care and nurture of His children should deal ruthlessly with their own sin (Mt. 18:6–9). They must cut out whatever would offend these paedobelievers. If their foot causes them to walk away from a needy covenant child to do more "important" tasks, they should chop it off. If their hand refuses to give to a child of the covenant what rightfully belongs to him, they should amputate it. If their eye looks the other way, ignoring the helplessness of the child, they should be quick to gouge it out. Children must be treated as insiders, with special reverence and respect. They are not second-class citizens of the kingdom. They should be served the same way we would serve an apostle, or even Christ Himself. If a Christian parent is devoted to *anything* more than to raising godly children, that parent is seriously out of step with Jesus' kingdom vision. Jesus makes it clear this is a matter of supreme significance.

Jesus goes on, in the following verses, to further explain the high standing He gives to covenant children. By nature, children are objects of wrath, but the covenant promise has transformed the children of believers into objects of grace. Thus, it is precisely these little ones He came to seek and save (18:10–14). Their (guardian?) angels have a special nearness to the heavenly Father. Unlike other angels, these do not cover their eyes in God's presence (cf. Isa. 6:2). Moreover, the fact that these children have angels ministering to them indicates that they are heirs of salvation (cf. Heb. 1:14). Apparently, while children may often be regarded as lowly on earth, they have special representation in the heavenly courts above.[7] Our care and concern for covenant children should be patterned after the angels: we should constantly intercede for them before the throne of grace and minister to them in whatever ways we can.

Verses ten through fourteen do not just describe a general, providential care exercised on behalf of covenant children. God loves these children as His own and desires their salvation (18:14). *Every* covenant child (every "sheep") is important to Him; He would gladly leave the fold of ninety-nine to pursue the *one* who wanders away from the rest. Our children are really *His* children (cf. Ezek. 16:20; Mal. 2:15), for they are members of His flock. Jesus strongly emphasizes the intense, personalized care He has for all the children of His people.

Certainly, then, if God gives these children such a privileged position, He desires to receive them at the baptismal font and feed them at His table. He treats them as believers, as full covenant members, and we should as well. He desires them to be a part of the life of the covenant community, including its sacramental life. Obviously, Jesus thought children could have a genuine relationship with God even apart from being able to verbalize propositional truth about Him. Jesus was no rationalist! Children may not be able to digest preaching cognitively, but nothing hinders them from receiving Jesus and entering His kingdom. Just as children were full members of the old covenant nation, so they are full citizens of Christ's new covenant kingdom. And they enjoy that citizenship *now*—before reaching a certain age or maturity level. Because of the covenant promise, they are born into the kingdom (or at least with a right to enter the kingdom in baptism).

All of this is very practical, of course. The way Jesus regards covenant children is the way we should regard them. Parents and pastors, especially, should take note, for here are the major keys we need to form our children into mature disciples of Christ. Parental nurture is all about

---

7. Jesus' words here about angels are obviously difficult to interpret. For an alternative explanation, see Warfield, "The Angels of Christ's 'Little Ones'," in *Shorter Writings*, vol. 1, 253ff. Warfield argues the "angels" of the children are actually their souls. That is to say, Jesus is indicating the children themselves have a place near God's throne. I think Warfield's view is a stretch exegetically, but it makes sense theologically.

character formation, and character formation is all about covenantal identity. Covenant children should be reminded that they are loved by God, perhaps just as often as they are reminded that they are loved by their parents. They should *not* be trained in methodological doubt or systematic skepticism, as some Christian parenting strategies have it. They should learn to think of God as their Father and Jesus as their Elder Brother[8] from their earliest days. They should be enculturated into the life of the kingdom from the beginning, constantly learning the privileges and responsibilities that have fallen to them as citizens in God's new messianic world. They should not be pressed for conversion, but should be exhorted to "improve" their baptisms, per the Westminster Longer Catechism (WLC) question 177. In doing these things, we give them a solid foundation on which to build a life of faithful service to Christ.

### Matthew 19:13–15

Matthew 18:1–14 is a rather comprehensive theology of covenant children, but Jesus has still more to teach us. In the following chapter, Matthew again picks up this thread in Jesus' ministry. This time little children are brought to Jesus for blessing. Jesus does not drive them

---

8. While the notion of God as Father to His covenant people gets at least some attention, Jesus as Elder Brother (or "firstborn"; see Rom. 8:29) has been largely neglected. And yet this would seem to be a valuable sanctification dynamic for parents to tap into as they raise their children. Typically, after they reach a certain age, children aspire to be like some "older brother" figure even more than like their parents. Thus, by presenting Jesus as the "Older Brother," we are giving children just what they crave—someone close enough to them to serve as a pattern, and yet also someone to "look up to," to view as a hero. If kids feel a deep urge to dress and act like older kids, parents should be quick to present Jesus as the "Older Kid," the ultimate example they should desire to emulate. Jesus is the true "Youth Pastor" to our children. This older brother motif could even serve as a helpful model in developing a pattern for youth ministry in the local church. The purpose of such ministry would not simply be fun and games, but shepherding children in the way of salvation unto maturity. Despite evangelicalism's amazing proliferation of "youth groups" over the last century, very little work has actually been done by the church to *disciple* children. When the Church tries to compete with the entertainments and allurements of the world, she always loses. It is time for the church to reconfigure youth ministry around a biblical theology of covenant children.

away, contrary to the disciples' expectations (19:13; note the disciples still have not learned the lesson!). Instead, He says, "Let the little children come to Me, and do not forbid them; for of such is the kingdom of heaven." Whereas the disciples wanted to put up a hedge to keep children out, Jesus invites them into His presence. There was something about Jesus that attracted children, just as He attracted other socially marginalized people and cultural outcasts.

We see here that Jesus was never too busy for children; indeed, they occupied a special place of prominence—or "greatness"—in His earthly ministry. Contrary to the disciples' wishes, Jesus invites little ones to Himself and relishes their company. He includes them as full members of His kingdom. The disciples rebuked those bringing their children to Jesus, but Jesus in turn rebuked the disciples. The disciples' (baptistic) vision of a kingdom without children is not going to be realized. Indeed, the kingdom can only be entered and maintained by those who are willing to become like children in humility and helplessness. The disciples are in danger of offending children precisely because they are offended by children (cf. 18:10–14; 19:13).

Jesus said little children were not forbidden to be brought before Him. This is a great encouragement to Christian parents. Jesus *wants* to meet our children. There is no entry age requirement for the kingdom; all are welcome. Jesus embraced these children, laying hands on them and giving them a benediction (cf. Mk. 10:16). By laying hands on them, blessing flows out from Him to the children (cf. Lk. 8:45).[9]

---

9. In Scripture, touch is frequently the medium through which divine blessing and curse flow. Touching is a major theme in Leviticus, since uncleanness spreads through contact (cf. Gen. 3:3; Lev. 5:2–3; 7:19, 21; 11:24ff, etc.). But we also find touch can serve as a means for transmitting favor (Gen. 27; 1 Ki. 7:21; 2 Ki. 4:34, etc.). In the gospels, we find the touch of Jesus reverses the flow of uncleanness. So Jesus can go around touching the unclean, and instead of contracting their defilement, His life and healing power overcome uncleanness and bring restoration (cf. Lk. 8:40–56). He stops up the flow of death and reverses it into a flow of life (cf. Rom. 5:12, 15–21).

How does Jesus touch our infants today? In other words, how can our children get what those children in Matthew 18 and 19 got? How can they be welcomed by Jesus into the kingdom? The blessing is extended primarily through the pastor as he acts in Jesus' name and as His representative, taking the child into his arms to baptize him and speak Christ's promises to him. Jesus touches

But here's the catch: blessings can only be received by faith. Why would Jesus offer and bestow a blessing unless these children have the requisite faculty needed to receive the blessing? Why offer something that could not be received in the nature of the case (assuming infant faith is impossible)? Again, this passage only makes sense if we view the children as little believers. They've entered the kingdom by faith; they represent Jesus by faith; they come to Jesus by faith; they receive His blessing by faith. In all these things, they are models for adults, not the other way around.[10]

The plot thickens when we look at Luke's version of the narrative. Luke identifies some of the children who were brought to Jesus specifically as *infants* (Lk. 18:15). These are not just toddlers or other small children who could hear the call of Jesus. These are helpless babes who had to be carried to Jesus. They were utterly dependent. They were explicitly pre-rational and pre-verbal children. Jesus' covenant welcome extends to the youngest of children. The vocabulary used in Matthew emphasizes the smallness of the children interacting with Jesus (*paidion* in Mt. 18:4, 19:13–14; the diminutive form of the normal word for children, *pais*; *micron* in 18:6, 10, 14). But Luke makes the case even stronger: his term, *brephos*, includes not only newborn infants, but even pre-born embryos. The welcome and blessing of Jesus extends even to children in the womb!

Nothing in Matthew 19:13–15 identifies these covenant children as

---

the child through water as He pours out His Spirit. But, of course, parents are also Jesus' representatives, and covenant children begin to experience the love of Christ in and through the love of their parents. When Jesus touched the children, He was sharing with them His own life and holiness; those blessings continue to be available to our covenant children as we nurture them in Christian discipleship, serving as Christ's instruments and agents. Just as the Spirit flowed out from Jesus to those He touched, so it is with us (cf. Lk. 8:46; Jn. 7:38). Of course, parents can only serve as effective agents of Christ's presence and blessing as they trust God's covenant promises about their children.

10. Infant baptism presupposes the same point: why offer to infants the blessings of Christ and His benefits in the waters of baptism if infants are constitutionally incapable of receiving those blessings through the exercise of faith? The Church has erred grievously in making adult baptism/faith the norm rather than infant baptism/faith. See Peter Leithart, "Infant Baptism in History: An Unfinished Tragicomedy," in *The Case for Covenantal Infant Baptism*, edited by Gregg Strawbridge (Phillipsburg, NJ: Presbyterian and Reformed, 2003), 246ff.

unique among the wider group. Apparently, Jesus intended His declarations about children and their covenant status as kingdom members
to be applicable to any covenant child, however young. These particular
children represent the rest of that class of persons. Jesus regards covenant infants and children as believers; we should as well.

Jesus' actions were radically counter-cultural. The disciples' views reflect a general first-century Jewish outlook that covenant children did not
*really* begin moving toward God's kingdom until age twelve, when Jewish
boys came under the full yoke of Torah. This was a kind of functional "age
of accountability" for Jews, but Jesus challenges this whole notion (along
with many other perversions of biblical teaching in first century Judaism).
Children who are brought to Him become members of the kingdom of
God, even if they are newborn infants. For Jesus, there is no age of accountability. He treated children with all the dignity of full personhood.
He regarded children as capable of Spiritual relationships.

Unfortunately, the attitude of the disciples toward little children is
still alive in the church today, even in Reformed circles. I have heard
Presbyterian elders say things like, "You can't expect anything spiritually good to come from a child until at least nine years old." But where
is this found in Scripture? Jesus clearly blessed children much younger
than that, including them in His kingdom. He did not give a shred of
evidence that children needed to reach a certain age before they could
enter into a relationship with Him. Instead, He treated all the covenant
children He encountered according to the Davidic paradigm in
Psalms 22 and 139. The same principle of infant faith/membership that
obtained in old covenant Israel continues to be operative in the eschatological new covenant kingdom.

Unfortunately, it is most often the men in the church who tend to
view children the way the disciples did rather than the way Jesus did.
Perhaps they are less likely to feel compassion toward the weakness and
vulnerability of children. It is not uncommon for men to think themselves above interacting with children, staffing the nursery, teaching
children's Sunday school classes, and so forth. If we order our church
life in light of Jesus' ministry to children, however, these services might,
in fact, be among the most important. We should all desire to befriend
the church's children, knowing that we can represent Jesus to them

even as they represent Jesus to us. We must learn to discern the face of Jesus in the faces of our covenant children.

## Other Texts

We have sketched out the major lines of evidence for paedofaith in the New Testament. Just to round out the discussion, we should note a few other places where we find Jesus speaking and acting favorably toward children. He healed children, often on account of their parents' faith (e.g., Mt. 10:18–26; 15:21–28; 17:14–21). His compassion for the plight of children has been unequalled in human history. He continually reached out to children in love and grace. This pattern was a major feature of His ministry and sets the course the church should follow.

Moreover, in Matthew 11:25, Jesus identifies "babes" as special recipients of heavenly revelation. These may be disciples of any age (metaphorically speaking), but certainly young children (literal "babes") are not excluded. Many children obviously received revelation from the Father about the identity of Jesus (Mt. 21:15; Lk. 1:41).

To sum up, at every point, Jesus goes out of His way to include children within the scope of His redemptive mission and give them an exalted place in His kingdom. Just as Jesus' gospel outlook revolutionized the ancient world's view of women and the poor, so He brought in a radically new way of welcoming and caring for children. His treatment of children is fully in line with the Old Testament, but goes even further, because now children are included not merely in the old covenant, but in the new and better eschatological covenant (the kingdom of God) Jesus came to inaugurate. The new form and shape of the covenant does not cut children out, but gives them first rank among the disciples. Indeed, covenant children stream into the kingdom ahead of the religious leaders of the day. May we have the grace to follow their lead (cf. Isa. 11:6).

three

## the mystery of paedofaith

God makes promises to our children. What is the content of those promises? *Nothing less than salvation.* He promises to be *their God* (Gen. 17:7),
which is just a shorthand way of saying He promises to be a personal
Lord and Savior to them. He promises to be *for them* in Christ Jesus. In
Jesus, we find God's supreme self-revelation of love directed toward
His people and their offspring. All the promises of God are "Yes!" and
"Amen!" in Him, including His promises to our children. In other
words, God has promised our children the riches of the gospel, namely,
Christ and His benefits. This includes giving them faith, even as infants.
To be sure, covenant children can grow up to reject this promised offer
just as their parents can. This apostasy is a sad and mysterious reality,
but God's promise is what it is—a trustworthy and sure pledge of forgiveness and new life in Christ.

To deny the possibility of infant faith is to deny the sovereignty of
God. It is to make human ability the measure of God's action. Geoffrey
Bromiley explains:

Since faith is the suprahuman operation of the Spirit, it can be given even when there is no normal consciousness of it and even when self-consciousness as such has not developed.

The faith which justifies and saves is not a human possibility, the work of flesh and blood, but a divine reality, the sovereign work of the Spirit, who does not find it at all impossible to reveal the things of God to babes. Indeed, as Luther also pointed out, it is no more a miracle for the Holy Spirit to work in the less resistant hearts of infants than it is for Him to work in the self-opinionated and sin-hardened hearts of adults. Precisely because of their self-conscious possibilities, adults are dead in trespasses and sins. For despite all their vaunted faculties, they have of themselves no understanding in this area. Only a rationalistic mind, even though it be the rationalistic mind of a believer, can foolishly suppose that adults enjoy some native possibility of faith whereas infants are such impossible subjects that even the Holy Spirit cannot begin His work in them if He so chooses, or indeed bring them to a real faith of which they will not have awareness until later years should they attain a full self-conscious life. Surely, the Holy Spirit laughs at this so-called possibility and impossibility, just as He laughs at all man's pretentious possibilities and all his solemn judgments on such impossibilities as the virgin birth or the resurrection of Christ from the dead. Who are we to tell the Holy Spirit what He can and cannot do?

In the instance of God's work in infants . . . we have an impossibility which He not only can do but according to the biblical records does do. Infants have in fact been the subjects of the sovereign operation of the Holy Spirit.[1]

God's capacity is not limited by the (in)capacities of infants. If faith is a gift of the Spirit, nothing hinders it being given to infants. There is no minimum level of intelligence or ability needed in order to be a fit recipient of God's gracious work.[2]

---

1. Geoffrey Bromiley, *Children of the Promise: The Case For Baptizing Infants*, 72–74. Bromiley goes on to cite several biblical examples: Jeremiah 1:5; Luke 1:15, 32–35; and Galatians 1:15.

2. My questions for those who deny the possibility of infant faith: What is the minimum IQ a person must have in order to be open to the working of God's Spirit? How do you know? What are the minimum intellectual and physical abilities a person must have? And how is a denial of God's freedom to work faith in the totally incompetent compatible with His sovereignty and with *sola gratia*?

Note that paedofaith in covenant children is not a "natural" inheritance, as though parents could pass on faith genetically. "God has no grandchildren," as the saying goes. Each new generation requires a fresh application of covenant grace.

Rather, we may say that God's work of redemption is embedded in the structures He set up at creation. Thus, God respects the natural order of the family and works through it. As one Puritan put it, "God has cast the line of election through godly loins." Children do not naturally have faith or the Spirit or even a right to baptism. They only have these things because of God's covenant promise and grace, but God's promise embraces nature in order to heal, perfect, and transform it, bringing it to its intended eschatological end.

The key is to see that God's sovereignty in salvation and the covenant promises made to families are not at odds. We cannot play God's sovereignty off against God's covenant. It is precisely because God is sovereignly redeeming His whole creation through the blood of Christ that the covenant promises can be trusted. Only a sovereign God committed to the comprehensive restoration of the fallen world order can make and keep promises that include the salvation of the children of His people.[3]

---

These are serious questions. In my opinion, denying infant faith has radical anti-gospel implications.

3. On the interrelationship between creation, redemption, and infant baptism, consult P. Richard Flinn's excellent article, "Baptism, Redemptive History, and Eschatology," in *The Failure of American Baptist Culture*, edited by James B. Jordan (Tyler, TX: Geneva Divinity School, 1982), 131–51. The Reformed antithesis is not between nature and grace but sin and righteousness. The new creation is as broad as the old creation. Every aspect of human reality (minus sin), including family and social life, is swept up into the new eon of Christ and will be transformed. Jesus said to baptize and disciple the nations, and nations include children (Mt. 28:18–20). This means children can be brought under the redemptive sway of Christ's lordship from their earliest days. This covenant participation in the new Israel comes to fruition through the rite of baptism. Christ is the Head of a new humanity, but that new humanity does not exclude children, as He made clear during His earthly ministry. The covenant blessings our children share in are not a natural possession, but an aspect of God's comprehensive, creation-embracing grace. If redemption is simply the restoration and glorification of creation as such, paedofaith and paedobaptism are logical necessities.

The data amassed thus far are enough to contradict the assertion of Paul Jewett that "the Bible *always* speaks of repentance and faith—those Siamese twins of grace—in terms of a change of mind, an enlightening of the understanding, a renewal of the will, which comes by hearing the Word and issues in a conscious commitment to Christ."[4] The Bible manifestly does *not* always speak of faith in such a way as consideration of Psalm 22:9, Psalm 71:5, and Matthew 18:6 indicate.[5] Faith is not always knowledgeable, intellectual, and verbal in Scripture; the biblical teaching shows that faith admits those of various maturity levels and degrees of cognitive comprehension and articulation. Infant faith is no less real than adult faith, even if it lacks some of the features we would demand in adults. Infant faith is personal trust; adult faith is personal trust plus propositional knowledge and assent. Yet the former deserves to be called "faith" every bit as much as the latter.[6] David says so, after all (cf. Ps. 22:9–10), and Jesus agrees (Mt. 18:6).

### Baptism, Paedofaith, and the Status of Infants

Several theological points follow from these insights and from the biblical passages we have surveyed. First, we need to explore the relationship of paedofaith to the efficacy of baptism. How do our children receive what is offered in baptism? Is baptism an efficacious sign to them? What is their status and state before, during, and after their baptism? Does paedofaith buttress the case for paedobaptism? When do our children become believers in relation to the timing of baptism? To help answer these questions we will draw on two of the greatest theologians in the Reformed tradition—John Calvin and Francis Turretin.

---

4. Jewett, 268, emphasis added.

5. Surprisingly (or perhaps not!), none of these passages appears in the Scripture index of Jewett's book.

6. Scripture quite often describes faith in terms of its propositional content (e.g., Rom. 10:9 and surrounding context; 1 Cor. 12:3). Such content is mandatory for adults since their knowledge of other persons always includes a propositional element. But it is not necessary for the more primal faith of infants. The passages that describe faith in terms of propositional content often have to do with missionary contexts and preaching. They cannot be forced upon our children any more than 2 Thessalonians 3:10.

The sacrament of initiation (circumcision in the old covenant, baptism in the new) effects a formal, public transition in the status of the child. At baptism, a definitive line is crossed. Whatever we say about the pre-baptismal faith of covenant children, the significance of this event should not be underestimated. Here we must be nuanced in order to be true to Scripture and the Reformed faith.

Calvin described the objective-yet-conditional efficacy of the sacraments in this way:

> Hence we see that sacraments are never destitute of the virtue of the Spirit unless when men render themselves unworthy of the grace offered in them. When papists speak of the efficacy of the sacraments they say that they are efficacious, if only we remove the obstacle of mortal sin: they make no mention of faith . . . We see how they are steeped in blindness, according to God's just judgment. We must hold, therefore, that there is a mutual relation between faith and the sacraments, and hence, that the sacraments are effective through faith. Man's unworthiness does not detract anything from them, for they always retain their nature. Baptism is the laver of regeneration, although the whole world should be incredulous (Titus 3:5) . . . but [without faith] we do not perceive the grace which is offered to us; and although spiritual things always remain the same, yet we do not obtain their effect, nor perceive their value, unless we are cautious that our want of faith should not profane what God has consecrated to our salvation.[7]

For Calvin, baptism is an efficacious offer of salvation to be received by faith. Lack of faith does not vitiate the sacrament considered in itself, but it does mean the one baptized receives the grace of baptism in vain. For Calvin, infant baptism was not an empty outward rite. Calvin believed baptism belonged to covenant children because they possess a seed of faith, which means they receive baptism in an appropriate way. Baptism does not create faith (as in Lutheran theology), but offers Christ to faith already present in the heart of the child. Because of this seed faith, the child makes right use of baptism. He is not an alien or stranger

---

7. Taken from Calvin's commentary on Ezekiel 20:20. See his *Commentary on the First Twenty Chapters of the Book of the Prophet of Ezekiel*, trans. by Thomas Myers (Grand Rapids, MI: Baker Book House, 1993 reprint), 311f.

to the sacrament because he already knows the One offered in the sacrament in an unformed way.

For Calvin, baptism is our entrance into the Church. The Church, as our holy mother, gives birth to us through the rite of baptism, completing our adoption and making us her children (*Institutes* 4.1.1). Of course, the promises are already applicable to the covenant child before baptism, and in fact secure the child's right to baptism. Nevertheless, baptism effects a real transition in the state and standing of the child. Baptism ratifies the child's place among God's people, seals to him the forgiveness of sins, and officially begins the lifelong process of regeneration. Calvin holds in (biblical, I would say) tension the blessings that belong proleptically to the child *before* baptism, and the blessings that become his in a new and transformed way *in* the sacrament itself. Infants are already regenerate and adopted *before* baptism in one sense, but receive regeneration and adoption *at* baptism in another, fuller sense. The movement is from grace to grace.[8]

Thus Calvin says, on the one hand, "God pronounces that He adopts our infants as His children *before they are born*, when He promises that He will be a God to us, and to our seed after us. This promise includes their salvation" (*Institutes* 4.15.20; emphasis added). Children already belong to the family of God in principle at conception (obviously before baptism). Calvin makes very strong statements to this effect.

---

8. Obviously, then, Calvin's doctrine of baptismal efficacy is richly nuanced. His view of efficacy is distinct from that of the Roman Catholic Church. Rome argues the sacraments work *intrinsically*, like medicine; Calvin emphasizes that God works through the sacraments *instrumentally*, as Christ and the Spirit make them effectual administrations of the covenant. Rome views the grace of the sacrament as a quasi-substance, poured into the one baptized, provided no mortal sin hinders its flow; Calvin views the sacraments as personalized signs through which grace (in the sense of God's attitude of favor and the working of His Spirit) is attested and sealed to believers. On the nuances of Calvin's view of covenant children before and after baptism and an effort to resolve—or at least lessen—the tension, see my essay "Calvin and the Efficacy of Infant Baptism" available at http://www.hornes.org/theologia/content/rich_lusk/calvin_and_the_ efficacy_of_infant_baptism.htm.

The offspring of believers are born holy, because their children, while yet in the womb, before they breathe the vital air, have been adopted into the covenant of eternal life. Nor are they brought into the church by baptism on any other ground than because they belonged to the body of the church before they were born. He who admits aliens to baptism profanes it . . . For how can it be lawful to confer the badge of Christ on aliens from Christ. Baptism must, therefore, be preceded by the gift of adoption, which is not the cause of half salvation merely, but gives salvation entire; and this salvation is afterwards ratified by Baptism.[9]

On the other hand, he says "baptism is a kind of entrance into the church; for we have in it a testimony that we who are otherwise strangers and aliens, are received, into the family of God, so as to be counted of His household" (*Catechism of the Church of Geneva*; this is almost identical to the opening sentence on baptism in *Institutes* 4.15.1). In *Institutes* 4.15.3, he emphasizes what happens at the moment of baptism:

We must realize that *at whatever time we are baptized, we are once for all washed and purged for our whole life*. Therefore, as often as we fall away, we ought to recall the memory of our baptism and fortify our mind with it, that we may always be sure and confident of the forgiveness of sins. (Emphasis added)

In other words, baptism is our means of entry into the house of God and a state of forgiveness. It is transitional and effective.

So our children belong to God before baptism and thus have a right to baptism. And yet this does not make baptism a mere symbol of a pre-existing relationship. It retains its efficacy as an instrument of justification and regeneration. For Calvin, neither side of this tension can be given up: our children belong to God at conception; our children are enrolled in God's family at baptism. Calvin seemed rather satisfied to allow the paradox to go unresolved. The tension is somewhat lessened if we learn to think of God's relationship with our children as dynamic and vital, rather than static. In Calvin's 1555 sermon on Deuteronomy 7:9–10, he connects the sacraments with God's corporate election

---

9. Quoted in Lewis Bevins Schenck, *The Presbyterian Doctrine of Children in the Covenant* (New Haven: Yale University Press, 1940), 13.

and life in the body of Christ (which would certainly include our baptized children). Our children are elected and called to participate in the
covenant, which is not just an external apparatus, but a genuinely gracious and effectual, albeit conditional, administration of the gospel.[10]

Similarly, Reformed scholastic Francis Turretin describes the instrumentality of baptism in this way:

---

10. Calvin writes: "Now then it is of God's free election that we have His
Word purely preached unto us and that we have His gospel and Sacraments.
And therein we have reason to confess that He has shown Himself liberal to us.
For by what title is the Gospel given to us, rather than to such as who make
greater account of themselves than we do and who are not inferior to us as in
respect of the world? Why does God pass over great kingdoms and principalities
and nations of renown and choose a little nook and a small number of people
[that is, Israel] so that His Word shall be preached there? When it rains upon us
and all the rest of the world abides still in drought, is it not to be concluded that
God has the liberty to do good to whom He desires? And is this not His only
love, to which we are then beholden? Yes. So then, when the Gospel is preached
in a place and it has the warrants that God gives men salvation (as when we have
Baptism and the Lord's Holy Supper ministered uncorruptly) we may say it is an
election that God makes. But yet for all that, in the meantime He holds to Himself those He thinks good, to the end that men should not trust to the outward
signs without faith and obedience, knowing that although we have been chosen
to be of the body of the Church, yet if we make not our profit of that election,
God can well enough cut us off again and reserve a final number to Himself.
And though there may be a great multitude of us who confess all with one
mouth that God has chosen us, yet we cannot therefore say that He confirms us
as His children unless we live in pureness of faith and have ratified that covenant
God has made with us. And so let us understand that God's liberality shows
itself in all kinds of ways to us, and that therefore we have greater cause to love
Him more and more and to yield Him all praise. For have we His Word? It is a
free gift to us, whereby He has bound us to Himself. Do we have His sacraments? They are the badges of His fatherly election. We have not deserved these
things . . . And so (as I said before) we see that in all respects we must keep our
mouths shut from bragging of anything." Taken from *Sermons on Deuteronomy:
Facsimile of 1583 Edition* (repr., Edinburgh: Banner of Truth Trust, 1987), 316–17,
spelling and wording updated. In Calvin's view, our children are part of the
corporately elect people; our children are to be baptized into Christ's body because the covenant belongs to them even before baptism. Calvin's catechetical
materials for children also treat them as Christians, in need of discipleship, not
initial conversion. This view of the child is rooted in baptism and the covenant,
and provides a platform for parental nurture, as we will see.

Although the sacraments are external means and instruments applying (on the part of God) the promise of grace and justification, this does not hinder faith from being called the internal instrument and means on the part of man for receiving this benefit offered in the word and sealed by the sacraments.

The question is not whether faith alone justifies to the exclusion either of the grace of God or the righteousness of Christ or the word and sacraments (by which the blessing of justification is presented and sealed to us on the part of God), which we maintain are necessarily required here . . . For all these as they are mutually subordinated in a different class of cause, consist with each other in the highest degree.[11]

According to Turretin, baptism is instrumental in offering salvation, and faith (alone) is instrumental in receiving it. These cannot be played off against each other because they subsist together in the covenant with the highest degree of harmony (along with other instruments and means). Baptism and faith are correlatives. Baptism is to faith what a gift is to the hand. The function of the hand (faith) is to latch onto the gift (baptism) and hold it securely. Without faith, the gift cannot be grasped. Of course, the gift of baptism is really the gift of Christ himself, sacramentally presented. As with Calvin, however, baptism does not create faith; rather it presupposes faith. Baptism is only used rightly when given to believers. The efficacy of baptism, even in the case of children, hinges on the presence of faith.

This comes into sharper focus as we examine Turretin's view of baptismal efficacy in relation to the guilt and presence of sin. Baptism does not work physically but morally and Spiritually, in the same way the Word works. Unlike Rome, which lodges the efficacy of the sacrament in the physical element itself and limits the effect of baptism to past and present sins, Turretin argues that the grace of baptism is found in a personal relationship of favor with God, which covers the whole of the believer's life. Thus, post-baptismal penance is not necessary to deal with ongoing sin; instead, believing sinners may call to mind again and

---

11. Taken from *Institutes of Elenctic Theology* (Phillipsburg, NJ: Presbyterian and Reformed, 1992), trans. by George Musgrave Geiger and edited by James T. Dennison, 16.7.20; 16.8.5.

again their baptisms in a spirit of faith and repentance. Turretin, in harmony with Calvin, says that "sin is taken away by baptism, that it is not imputed, nor does it reign; nor also that it ceases to be. Therefore we hold that guilt is indeed fully taken away, but pollution only incipiently and partly." In other words, the sacrament offers a full and final justification (since guilt is an all or nothing proposition), and commences sanctification (since removal of sin's filth is a progressive process).

Rome had argued that baptism removes original sin, returning one to an Adamic state of original righteousness, but this righteousness can be lost. The Reformers, such as Calvin and Turretin, argued that baptism does indeed remit original sin, but also all actual sin. More than that, it bestows upon us not merely Adamic righteousness, but Christ's righteousness. Thus, the Reformers actually held a much higher and stronger view of baptism than the Roman Church.

Turretin, like Calvin, insists that baptism is an efficacious sacrament. It is efficacious because of Christ's word and the Spirit's work; it is efficacious through faith and not merely the absence of mortal sin. The twofold grace of baptism is rooted in union with Christ, and includes washing from sins and entrance into newness of life. In the believing reception of baptism, Christ Himself is applied and conferred.

> When Scripture says that sins are cleansed, purged, destroyed and washed away in baptism (Eph. 5:26; Titus 3:5), this must be understood not physically but sacramentally; not absolutely with respect to all the baptized, but only with respect to those who believe (Mk. 16:16). The cleansing and blotting out must be understood according to the nature of the thing (with respect indeed to guilt, full and perfect), while with respect to inherent pollution, inchoate and successive as to existence.[12]

In summary, baptism absolves sin altogether and breaks the back of reigning sin so that a life of faithful obedience can begin. In principle, this is what both adults and infants receive in the administration of baptism.

Turretin views baptism as the offer of salvation and the point of entry into the church. The Spirit works through an external sign to ratify

12. Turretin, 19.1.4.

and apply the promises of the covenant. Baptism is simply the gospel in sacramental form, offered to faith.

In *Institutes* 19.20.5–6, Turretin says that children are to be baptized because the essence of the covenant belongs to them. God is their God; therefore, they are to be received into His family. Covenant succession is built into the covenant itself. Turretin, like Calvin, insists that children of believers already belong to God in some sense even before baptism, though he does not allow this to vitiate the efficacy of the sacrament. He says infants are to be baptized because "to infants belong the thing signified (to wit, remission of sins, regeneration, the kingdom of heaven)." He goes on to connect this to Spirit–wrought paedofaith: "What hinders them from being called holy and believers by the Holy Spirit given to them, although they cannot as yet exert an act of [rational] faith?"[13]

Like Calvin, Turretin says nothing definitive about *how* God actually works on the heart and mind apart from or through an external instrument. We are told Christ and the Spirit use the outward sign as an instrument to offer the gospel to faith, but the formation of faith prior to baptism and the efficacy of the sacrament itself are largely mysterious.

What can we say to this data? In the case of infants, paedofaith means that initiation into the covenant at baptism serves to formalize and solemnize a relationship which had *already* begun even prior to baptism.[14] If baptism is the place where the child officially "marries" Christ (cf. the language of union with Christ in connection with baptism in Romans 6:3ff and the baptismal washing language in connection with marriage in Ephesians 5:26), prior to baptism the child is betrothed to

13. Unfortunately, Turretin, in the end, hedges on infant faith much more than Calvin. See Turretin, *Institutes* 19.20.18–19. However, no matter how many qualifications he throws in, he is willing to admit some form of seed faith to covenant children: "The same thing must be said of the faith of covenanted infants as of their reason. Each is in them in the first act, not in the second; in the sowing, not in the harvest; in the root, not in the fruit; in the internal power of the Spirit, not in the external demonstration of work." This ensures they receive an efficacious baptism. In chapter six, we will look more closely at Turretin's nuanced view of infant faith.

14. The covenant promise is God's welcome mat on the front porch of His house. In baptism, the child actually passes through the doorway into the house itself. But even before baptism the child is in the process of being adopted into the Lord's family.

Christ. During the "engagement period" (from conception up until baptism) the child is loved by Christ and has a real relationship with Him. The child has a word of promise from the Lord of the covenant, a word that will come to even greater fruition when the child is brought for formal initiation into the covenant people. At baptism, the child's faith is given something tangible to lay hold of, and he enters publicly and officially into God's covenant community (1 Cor. 12:13). In this way, baptism strengthens and increases the faith of the child (cf. Westminster Confession of Faith [WCF] 14.1). The child's pre–baptismal faith means he is able to receive what God offers to him in baptism, namely, Christ and the promise of forgiveness through participation in His death and resurrection. Paedofaith prevents us from viewing paedobaptism as an empty, outward sign. It ensures that the child's baptism is efficacious, not empty.[15]

Baptism, then, does *not* create faith in the heart of the child (as the Lutherans sometimes claim). Rather, through faith the child *receives* what God *offers* in baptism, namely, Christ and the benefits of the new covenant (Westminster Shorter Catechism [WSC], questions 88, 91–95). Through faith, the child grows to internalize the objective status and identity bestowed upon him by baptism as a member of the kingdom of Christ and the house and family of God (WCF 25.2). In baptism, faith is confirmed and assured, even in the case of infants. But faith still must grow to maturity, ever more embracing what was given and received in baptism. Exactly *how* all of this happens in children is not exactly spelled out in any detail in the Scriptures or by the great Reformed theologians, so we cannot answer all the questions we might be inclined to ask. This mystery is our next topic. But even as we probe the mystery, we must not lose sight of the points made thus far: our children have faith from the womb, even *before* being baptized; *at* baptism that faith is formed and confirmed in a new way (the same way a marriage ceremony formalizes and strengthens the relationship between a boyfriend and girlfriend); and *after* baptism the child must grow up into what was

---

15. This does not amount to a doctrine of baptismal regeneration, at least as it is understood by most evangelicals. See my essay "Do I Believe in Baptismal Regeneration?" available at http://www.auburnavenue.org/Articles/ do%20i%20 believe%20in%20baptismal%20regeneration.htm.

conferred in the sacrament, becoming more and more what his baptism says that he already is.[16]

## The Work of the Spirit and the Psychology of Faith

Second, nowhere does the Bible attempt to give a psychological explanation for infant faith.[17] As just admitted above, we are not told *how* infants can exercise faith, or precisely *how* God's relationship with them is constituted before baptism. How God works in the infant mind and heart is simply not a part of God's revelation to us and there is not much hope that scientists or psychologists will be able to help out here in a definitive and totally satisfactory way (cf. Ecc. 11:5). As we explore this mystery of paedofaith, we must learn to walk by faith, not trusting our own experience or reason, but the covenant declarations of Scripture.

The Lutherans usually speak here of God creating faith in the child *ex nihilo* at baptism. Yet that hardly answers the question and doesn't seem to square with David's claims to have faith even in the womb. We simply are not told anything about the means God uses to relate to infants *in utero* or form faith in their hearts. At most we can surmise that

---

16. In recent years renewed attention has been given to the high views of baptismal efficacy espoused by the Reformers. Of course, this retrieval project has met with stubborn resistance from some quarters. We cannot pause to defend a strong doctrine of baptismal efficacy here, so the quotations given above will have to suffice.

For a more contemporary account of baptismal efficacy, see Colin Gunton's superb article "Baptism and the Christian Community" in *Incarnational Ministry: The Presence of Christ in Church, Society, and Family*, edited by Christian D. Kettler and Todd H. Speidell, 98–109. Gunton's article is one of the finest brief treatments of baptism (including paedobaptism) I have ever read. It deserves careful study. Though occasionally more politically correct than biblically faithful, James F. White's book *The Sacraments as God's Self-Giving* (Nashville: Abingdon, 1983) is packed with provocative and practical insights into sacramental issues. White provides a compelling account of sacramental efficacy, tying the sacraments into the communal life of the Church. For an examination of baptismal efficacy from the vantage point of classical, evangelical Presbyterianism, see Craig Higgins' thesis paper, "The Washing of Regeneration: Baptismal Theology Among Ministerial Candidates in the Presbyterian Church in America," available at http://www.trinitychurch.cc/pdf/CRHThesis.pdf.

17. See Geoffrey Bromiley, *Children of the Promise: The Case For Baptizing Infants*, 70–71. Bromiley happily admits the mystery involved.

God works through the parents in a mysterious fashion to communicate Himself to the child (cf. Ps. 22:9).

Scripture does not provide a psychology of the Spirit's work. We know that He works apart from external signs at times, as well as through external signs, in accord with the biblical promises; but infant faith is a mystery. The Bible asserts it, but does not explain it. It does no good to argue for or against infant faith on the basis of claims about what we think infants can and cannot do. Infants, in Scripture, are said to actually have faith, and we must be willing to leave it at that. Their faith is strengthened and sealed in the sacrament of baptism and nurtured afterwards through other ecclesial and familial means, but we cannot say a whole lot about how it all works.

Some theologians have offered helpful insights into the nature of relationships extremely young children are capable of (e.g., recognizing the voice of mother and siblings while still in the womb), but still no exhaustive account of infant faith is possible, whether theological or scientific.

This mystery does not mean we should reject the doctrine. Even if we cannot articulate what it *really* means to claim infants have faith, we must also admit that we cannot explain what it means for God to be Triune or for the Son of God in human flesh to die on the cross. If someone is seeking to escape mystery, they need to find another religion, because Christianity is full of mysteries.

Besides, paedofaith may not really be any more enigmatic or unexplainable than adult faith. There is also great mystery in the way God works in the minds and hearts of adults. Since the psychological details of how God works in adults are not told to us, we cannot require a doctrine of paedofaith to give such an account in the case of infants. While God certainly does not usually bypass the mind in drawing an adult sinner to himself, there is still much about adult conversion that remains mysterious to us. After all, it is *both* a sovereign work of God *and* a free act of man. How does God cause a sinner to "come most freely, being made willing by his grace" (WCF 10.1)? How can the will be "free" yet "made willing" at the same time? How does God persuade the will of the sinner to embrace Christ by faith, without exercising "force" or "compulsion"? We're simply not told. With infants, we might wonder: how can a child have a relationship with another person when it is impossible for the child to interact through intelligible words and gestures? Again, we cannot say much about this.

The best attempt at defining and explaining paedofaith that I have found is set forth by Gottfried Hoffmann. Hoffmann seeks to make biblically appropriate use of child psychology:

> This claim [that children cannot believe because they cannot grasp preaching] certainly holds good with regard to the proclamation of the Gospel; but the very words of Christ make it yet more certain that little children are nevertheless in a position to receive the Kingdom of God and to have in their heart a relationship of trust to God and Christ. Is this not, however, precisely the decisive element of faith? For the fact that the child cannot yet put this personal relationship of trust into words does not at all mean that it is flatly incapable of it. Nor does it mean, furthermore, that this personal relationship of trust can only come about where conscious words and articulated speech can already be used.
>
> We ask leave at this juncture to make reference to certain insights of child psychology—not in order to thereby render the Lord's words acceptable, but to afford a little aid to understanding. We know today how children—and not they only—take in many things without their needing to be verbally articulated, without the use of consciously understood words. How it experiences its detachment from its mother at birth, how people treat it in the first days, weeks, and months (including what is given verbally), is absorbed by the child in a way which will determine its entire life. Thus already from birth onward there comes into existence a personal relationship to the "relational person" of the mother, whom it is thoroughly capable of distinguishing from other people. The child is capable of a "primal trust," and where this is not developed but held back, it sustains severe personality damage. This "primal trust" is not first developed through heard and understood articulated words, but in a personal mode which is other than verbal and can indeed dispense with the verbal dimension. A child "knows" that it is loved and whom it can trust long before it can understand the words "I love you." Thus it is a person also capable of personal relationship even without its being able to use intelligence and articulated words.[18]

---

18. Hoffmann, 88.

The argument of Hoffmann does not eliminate mystery from the nature of infant faith, but it does perhaps help make it more plausible. We need to think of infant faith in terms of a theology of personal relationships. Infant faith is a matter of personal relations, not discursive reflection. Still, the nature of faith accommodates itself to this form of interpersonal trust, even if we insist that in rationally capable people, faith includes propositional elements.

Nevertheless, the mystery remains. We cannot explain how infants come to have faith other than saying God simply turns their hearts to Himself. The psychology of the Spirit's work is ultimately elusive to us. Our minds can no more catch hold of how the Spirit works than our hands can catch hold of wind, water, oil, or flame.

## Infant and Adult Faith: What's the Difference?

Third, building upon what we have just noted, infant faith can be distinguished from adult faith just as an acorn can be distinguished from an oak tree or a newborn calf from a mature bull. At the core of each form of faith, however, is a trusting personal relationship with God. The traditional Reformed definition of faith as knowledge, assent, and trust makes adults rather than children the norm, which is fine as far as it goes, provided this norm is not absolutized. Clearly, David and Jesus did not absolutize adult faith. Admittedly, paedofaith cannot include factual knowledge in the same way as adult faith, though I do not think this overthrows our understanding of faith because the core is always the same: relational trust. While infant and adult faiths are different in various respects, to be sure, it is a difference of degree, not kind. Faith grows toward maturity as the total person grows. Infant faith lacks factual knowledge but retains personal knowledge, which is the heart and essence of saving faith.[19] Their faith is not discursive or reflective; rather it is

---

19. See Hoffmann, 89–91, for a fuller discussion. Hoffmann suggests that denying faith can exist without factual knowledge in the case of infants risks making faith dependent on articulation. This would not only exclude infants from faith, but would also call into question the mentally handicapped, the senile, and the dying. This is too steep a price to pay for absolutizing an intellectual definition of faith. Hoffmann's argument is helpful. "The child which receives or accepts the Kingdom of Heaven accepts this one Jesus of Nazareth and stands in a personal relationship of trust to this Jesus Christ and to no other. Perhaps an-

intuitive and (because of the Spirit's work) instinctive. It is not conscious, but infants do not have to be conscious of their faith in to order to have it. After all, they are not conscious of *any* of their members or faculties—though they still possess them nonetheless. Children are alive without "knowing" it as a matter of cognitive assent or rational reflection; in the same way they can have relational faith without being able to reflect on that fact or analyze it. They know and trust their mothers even from before birth, even though they do not know or assent to any propositions about them. As Hoffmann says, the child "believes and hangs on the Christ of the Creed without its knowing the Creed. As the child grows, though, there must also be a growth in the realm of knowledge, if that personal relationship of trust in Christ is not to be destroyed."[20]

As we saw from Matthew 18 and 19, infant faith has a kind of normativity of its own when we consider the kingdom from the standpoint of entrance. Paedofaith is protological; adult faith is eschatological. Paedofaith is initiatory; adult faith is consummational. Paedofaith is real faith, but mature adult faith is the final goal. The seed of infant faith has as its *telos* the full-grown, fruitful faith of an adult. The one is the *alpha* point of

---

other comparison may be helpful here. When a newborn child is placed on its mother's breast and perceives her heartbeat, it knows its mother, even though it lacks the knowledge that she has a particular shape, lives in a particular town, was born on a particular day and has experienced a particular destiny. If it remains with its mother, it will (in a certain sense, it must) get to know all these things, but already at birth it has thoroughly laid hold of this its mother, and stands in a full personal relationship to her. In a similar way, a child below the age of reason can also stand in a relationship to God and Christ, it can receive and accept Him, and this without knowing what He has done, being ignorant of the detailed features of His Person and Work."

This opinion [that infants cannot have faith because they lack intellectual and verbal abilities] narrows down man's capacity for a relationship with Christ and for accepting the kingdom of God by making it dependent on articulated understanding in a way which does not correspond with the actual working of Christ. At the same time it identifies the concept of personal relationship with linguistic articulation and with conscious decision, thereby curtailing the reality of personal human existence. (Might this be a delayed effect of the Greek definition of man as the being possessed of language?)" The child's relational knowledge will eventually mature into a more robust and comprehensive factual knowledge. But in the meantime, we still must regard the faith of the child to be genuine.

20. Hoffmann, 91.

faith; the other is its *omega* point. Our theology of faith must take into
account the nature of faith in its beginning, progress, and final form.

## Paedofaith and Saving Faith

Fourth, it should also be noted that not all infant faith is saving faith in the
sense of *persevering* faith.[21] This is another critical distinction. We already

---

21. In other words, we are not here saying that every covenant child is eternally elected to salvation. That much is obvious from Scripture and experience.
Our children are all elected (at the very least) to belong to the covenant in history, but not all covenant members have been chosen for perseverance to the end
and to eternal life. Some, sadly, break covenant, and their historical election de-
volves into eternal reprobation.

God has planned whatsoever comes to pass, including who will be saved
and lost, and who will persevere and who will apostatize. However, we must
beware of allowing eternal election to control the discussion of covenant children
because we do not have access to God's decretal will. We must order church and
family life by the covenant administration He has revealed to us in the deposit of
Scripture (Deut. 29:29), not by guesses about His secret plan. Covenant declarations about our children are *promises*, not *premises*; in other words, they are assertions to be grasped by faith, not axioms to be plugged into a logical system from
which we deduce eternal election. Parents should derive responsibilities and
privileges from the covenant affirmations, but we cannot deduce from these
affirmations eternal election unto salvation. We must judge the intentions of God
toward our children from His revealed will since this is all we have access to (Mt. 18:10–14).

The fact that not all paedofaith is saving faith should not unsettle Christian
parents, but should help them guard against presumption and laxity. Our calling
is to nurture paedofaith into strong, mature, persevering faith so our children can
make their calling and election sure. We are to trust God in this matter and make
use of all His appointed means. In the meantime, so long as our children have
not apostatized or been excommunicated, we have every right to *consider* them
eternally elect the same way we would any adult professing Christian walking
faithfully in the Church community.

This fact that not all paedofaith turns out to be saving faith should also not
be used to undercut comfort given to parents who have lost a covenant child in
infancy. My point in the next chapter is that covenant infants who die in infancy
did not evidence any signs of apostasy and so we have no reason to doubt their
eternal election. In such cases, all we can do is judge God's will from His Word—
and His Word to them includes promises of salvation. As Calvin says in *Institutes* 4.15.20, "The mere promise of God ought to be sufficient to assure us of the
salvation of our children." To fret over their salvation because they did not grow
up to manifest fruit or make a profession is to doubt the very Word of God. We

noted in our comments on Matthew 18:6ff that some infants will fall away. Some infants, like some adults, only believe for a season. In this case their faith may be regarded as one of the "common operations of the Spirit" (WCF 10.4; note that "common" in this context refers not to "common grace" given to believer and unbeliever alike, but to gifts of the Spirit held in common by elect and non-elect covenant members). They believed in vain (cf. 1 Cor. 15:2) and made shipwreck of their faith (1 Tim. 1:19). Obviously, non-elect infants will never have saving faith in a full, robust, persevering form. Meanwhile, elect infants, however much their faith may ebb and flow over the years through life's vicissitudes, will never completely abandon the covenant.

This is true of baptized infants as well. All baptized infants are offered Christ. The same water washes over all. Baptism, as a work of God, is never in vain. Like the Word, it always does what God wills in an ultimate sense (cf. Isa. 55:10–11). And yet, in the mysterious plan of God, some baptisms issue in eternal salvation, and others result in greater damnation. We cannot say why this is so from God's perspective, other than to remember that He is always just, holy, and loving, and always does all things for His own glory and purposes.

We can say why this is so from a human perspective. Some receive baptism to their profit because they receive it in faith that perseveres. Others do not receive baptism properly, either because they have no faith or they do not have lasting faith. In other words, baptism's efficacy unto salvation is conditioned ultimately on God's decree, but proximately on our response.

Remembering this prevents us from falling into a careless laxity about children. Ordinarily, if God has decreed for a child to persevere in faith, he has also appointed all the means suited to that end. Diligent parental nurture is one of the key means that prepares a child for a life of faithful and fruitful kingdom service. Parents should not obsess over the fact that they cannot peer into God's decretal will for their children. Instead they should claim the revealed covenant promises about their children and get to work!

---

can be as certain of their salvation as of any other Christian who dies in good standing in the Church. That's all we can ask for.

## Paedofaith and Theological Legalism

Finally, those who deny the possibility of infant faith often confuse the *presence* of faith with its *articulation*. Infants (and senile or mentally deficient persons, for that matter) may possess faith (in the sense of a trusting relationship with God), *despite* their verbal inability to express that faith. But God's arm is not too short to save; He can redeem to Himself even those whose mental abilities are too weak and/or immature to manifest their faith in intelligent, propositional form. Ordinarily, paedofaith should grow into knowledgeable, articulated faith, but such features are not of the essence of faith. Or, to put the matter another way, God's gift of faith is not dependent on our intellectual and verbal abilities, as though God could only give faith to people with a minimum IQ.

To deny this verges on turning faith into an autonomous human work. It is rationalism with a vengeance. Infants have a faith they cannot put into words, but it connects them with God and His kingdom nonetheless. (I would add: adults cannot put the totality of their faith into words either, so once again, while we may distinguish paedofaith from adult faith, they are on a continuum. Adults often have a relational trust in Christ that dwarfs their factual knowledge.)

If Christianity is an ideology, then infants are excluded. If Christianity is a new creation, a new life, a new community, a new relationship, a new Israel, then infants can be members as much as anyone else. To be sure, doctrine and ideas are critical; the church cannot survive apart from truth. The church must continually study and proclaim God's Word in an intelligent fashion. The church must cultivate the life of the mind and disciple the minds of her members, but *all of us* are growing into an understanding of God's truth. None of us has it all figured out. If Christianity depends on how much we can understand and articulate, or on our theological precision and formulations, it is just another form of legalism. Paedofaith is actually a helpful safeguard against an insidious tendency to imply salvation is by works—in this case the "work" of knowing theology or articulating biblical truth. There are some men in the Reformed church who need to be reminded that God can save people who have never read Berkhof's systematic theology.

## Evangelical Objections

Despite the biblical and theological case made above, evangelicals still sit uneasy with this doctrine of paedofaith. Two basic objections crop up, and we want to address them here.

### Paedofaith and Presumptions

First, it is assumed that a doctrine of paedofaith will lead to the worst kind of presumption and carelessness among parents and pastors, with the result that the church will be stuffed full of baptized unbelievers who have a false sense of assurance.

This objection is not just hypothetical. Consider the Church of England in England, where millions live as baptized unbelievers. In John Newton's day (1801), he could write, "I am told there are about ten thousand parishes in England; I believe more than nine thousand of these are destitute of the gospel." Now Newton may have been judging the Church too rigorously, or by too narrow a definition of the gospel, but any observer of the Church of England would have to admit that the body has had a high number of unfaithful members for a long time now. According to a 1999 estimate, the Church boasted some twenty-six million baptized members, though less than one million attended services with any regularity. The case of J. I. Packer illustrates the problem. Packer was baptized and confirmed in an Anglo-Catholic context, but testifies to having had no saving knowledge of Christ at the time. Indeed, after his conversion experience, he was angry with the Church of England for not telling him of his need for conversion all along. They were, in his eyes, only confirming him in the road to hell.[22]

The objection, then, is that a doctrine of paedofaith confuses birth into a Christian home and baptism with the experience of new birth and conversion, yielding a church full of hypocrites. A twofold response is in order. 1) While Packer blames the Church for not teaching him of his need to be converted, it seems it would be more biblical for him to blame the Church for failing to nurture him in the trust of his youth. A doctrine of paedofaith does not mean our children are saved no matter how they

---

22. Ian Murray, *Evangelicalism Divided* (Edinburgh: Banner of Truth Trust, 2000), 102–3.

live when they grow up. Rather, it means the faith God has given to covenant children must be nurtured and matured, lest it wither and die. Paedobaptism is not a free pass to heaven, but entrance into a conditional union with Christ that must be received and maintained by faith.

So, while the paedofaith paradigm will not stress the need for *a point* of conversion, it will stress the need for *a life* of ongoing conversion. A biblical doctrine of paedofaith will not fill the church with unfaithful members. Rather, it is a challenge to parents and children alike to live out what they've been given in the glorious covenant of grace. Evangelical fervor and devotion are not incompatible with paedofaith or efficacious sacraments. (If so, the original Reformers were not evangelicals). The paedofaith/paedobaptism link need not lead to nominalism, but should instead lead to a life of deep gratitude for the magnitude of God's saving grace.

2) The other answer to the baptized-but-unfaithful issue is simultaneously simple and hard. It is simple: apply church discipline; do not tolerate flagrant moral sin or heretical doctrine; only baptize the children of parents who can make a credible promise to nurture their children in the faith.

But it is also hard: any pastor will tell you that church discipline is easier to talk about than to do, especially when the problem has reached monumental proportions as in the Church of England or the Protestant mainline in America. It helps if non-attending members are finally regarded as self-excommunicated, but the real need of the hour is for churches to deal with the sin in their midst and on their rolls. One test of ecclesial fidelity is clearly our willingness to kick people out when the need arises (Rev. 2–3). It may be more painful for pastors than getting drawn and quartered, but it still must be done. (Those who don't feel this kind of holy reluctance about discipline probably aren't qualified to engage in it.)

*Paedofaith and Apostasy*

The second objection comes from the other side. If paedofaith is real faith, but not necessarily saving faith, doesn't that mean apostasy is a real possibility? And if apostasy is a real possibility, isn't that a denial of the perseverance of the saints? Doesn't it make assurance impossible? What good is paedofaith if it can be lost?

This is not the place to develop a full theology of apostasy. That has been done elsewhere.[23] The short answer is that the Bible does indeed teach that apostasy is a reality. There is such a thing as temporary faith. The warnings about falling away are not merely hypothetical. From God's perspective, all His people elected to eternal salvation will persevere in faith to the end. From our perspective, however, we cannot see the roll call of the elect, so we must go by what we can see (Deut. 29:29): covenant promises, verbal professions, outward obedience, participation in the life of the church, etc. Those who participate in the covenant only for a season do not fall away from eternal election, but they do fall away from the body of Christ, the kingdom of God, the corporate temple of the Holy Spirit, and so on. They shared in real blessings, and have now lost those blessings because of unbelief.

The threat of apostasy does *not* mean God's elect can be lost, it does *not* mean we actually persevere in our own strength rather than through faith by grace, and it does *not* mean we must give up all assurance of salvation. It simply means that we have to be vigilant and diligent. We have to keep our eyes focused on Christ at all times (Heb. 12:1–4), and we must train our children's eyes to stay locked onto Christ as well. That is the whole essence of our calling as Christians and as parents.

*Theoretically*, we can say no elect person will be lost. The number of the elected-unto-salvation can neither be increased nor diminished because God has fixed it in eternity past and works that plan out in history. However, under the providence of God, the life history of a reprobate person can include being born into a Christian family, having a form of faith as a child, being baptized into Christ, and later (for any number reasons) turning away from that covenant relationship. He may share for a time in quasi-redemptive blessings that analogously resemble those truly redemptive blessings the elect enjoy forever (cf. Heb. 6:4–6). Not everyone who is baptized shares in Christ's work in the same way

---

23. See my essay "New Life and Apostasy: Hebrews 6:4–8 as a Test Case" in *The Federal Vision*, eds. Steve Wilkins and Duane Garner (Monroe, LA: Athanasius Press, 2004), 271–98.

or to the same degree. Union with Christ, like any other relationship, is capable of an almost infinite number of permutations and particularities. There is one baptism, but a wide variety of ways of receiving and responding to baptism. Some ways lead to salvation, others do not.

Think of marriage as an analogy. All married people enter into the same kind of relationship, objectively speaking. There are certain privileges, obligations, and so forth that *all* married people cross into on their wedding day. Though from that point forward, any number of things could happen. Every couple has their own story. Some marriages are "happily ever after." Some marriages have ups and downs for a while, but finally settle down into a peaceful state. Others are rockier and end in disaster. They make shipwreck of their marriages; they receive the grace of marriage in vain; they partake of marriage but only temporarily. Of course, these are precisely the ways Scripture describes apostasy from the covenant.

*Practically*, whether one believes in apostasy or not, our responsibilities are the same. We must persevere to the end. We must obey. We must live a life of faithfulness. We must keep trusting Christ, relying on the Spirit, attending to the outward means of salvation, etc. So long as we reject antinomianism, we would all insist that covenant members must be covenant keepers in order to be saved, whatever theological mechanism we would use to describe those who, at one time, are part of the visible church and then later depart from it.

Assurance does not change either: we are only certain we know Christ as we turn away from self-reliance in order to trust him. Assurance is definitely possible, and the possibility of apostasy cannot negate that. Indeed, assurance is an intrinsic feature of faith. As we look to Christ, we come to know ourselves as forgiven sinners. Further, we see (with varying degrees of clarity) the fruits of faith in our lives in the form of theological orthodoxy, love for neighbor, and so on. By passing these "tests" we gain additional layers of assurance.

As I said earlier, not all paedofaith is saving faith. Parents come to know if their child has saving faith (rather than temporary faith) as he grows up and bears fruit or falls away. This same dynamic is true for new adult converts, and indeed for all Christians. The proof is in the persevering.

Faithful parents know that diligent parental care, discipline, nurture, teaching, training, and so on are God's appointed means for *keeping* our paedobelievers walking in the path of salvation all their days. A parent who knows that a) his child has faith from the outset, and b) that that faith is susceptible to disease and even death, will strive to do everything he can to ensure the health and vitality of his child's faith. He will feed that faith on the promises, commands, and warnings of God's Word, pray continually for the child, set for him a holy example, and surround him with the sacrificial love of Christ.

### What About Adoption?

One *might* get the impression from all that has been said that paedofaith and paedobaptism are realities that belong solely to the natural or biological family. After all, what else could David mean when he speaks of faith in the womb and at his mother's breast? His faith is obviously rooted in and linked to his membership in a natural family that possesses faith.

This impression is mistaken. Paedofaith and paedobaptism are first and foremost *covenantal* realities. The only reason the family matters is because the covenant promises are made to and embrace the family, but the promises are not based on bloodlines or genetics. They are based on the grace of Christ and the work of the Spirit. If paedofaith was strictly a matter of family heredity, why bother with the sacrament of baptism at all? Natural generation would be sufficient; there would be no need for supernatural regeneration—that is, a new birth that goes beyond anything the natural family can give. Baptism, properly understood, is the rejection of all forms of familiocentrism, because it witnesses to the inadequacy and fallenness of the family. The family has no power in itself. It stands in need of grace that comes from outside itself, so that family nurture can become a secondary means of grace. The primary means of grace (Word and sacrament) belong uniquely to the church, but a family that has been grafted into the church can become an instrument of grace as well. Jesus came to judge the natural family (e.g., Mk. 3:31–35; Mt. 10:34–38) and create the new, eschatological family of the church. But obviously the old, Adamic family structure can enter into the church; indeed, Jesus even called for whole nations to be brought into the church (Mt. 28:18–20).

Thus, God respects His own work of creation such that the "supernatural" comes through the natural. In other words, God's grace (His attitude of favor and His gifts) is communicated through creational means. The "matter" of creation is drawn up into the covenant of grace and therein becomes the substance of redemption and new creation. The family is fallen, but grace is promised to believing families to bring about restoration and healing. This is the rationale behind infant baptism. Infant baptism subordinates the family to the church in the economy of redemption, but it also indicates that the family structure is included in the scope of redemption. God sanctifies familial bonds.

With this framework in view, we are in a better position to assess the case of an adopted child. Let us suppose a Christian family adopts a child from non-Christian parentage. Does the child adopted into the Christian home receive the gift of paedofaith? Should he be baptized?

We answer with an emphatic "Yes!" to both questions. There is a biblical analogy here: in the old covenant, the household extended not just to blood relatives, but also to servants of the house (Gen. 17:12–13). For example, servants would have been circumcised and included in the Passover because they were regarded as members of their master's family (Ex. 12:43–51). They were under his covenant umbrella. Because he had authority over them, he was responsible for their care, including their covenant nurture and instruction in the true religion. By joining their master's family, they had a right to join Israel's family in circumcision.

So the household/family itself is not based on blood relationships but on covenant relationships. If old covenant servants were included under the provisions and promises of the covenant, how much more so a child adopted into a Christian home in the new covenant! That child is networked into the covenant through this new connection with believing family members. The promises and benefits now belong to the adopted child. He has been brought within the sphere of covenant mercies. Thus, on the basis of the covenant promises and the fact that the child will be discipled, he should be baptized.

When does an adopted child receive paedofaith? I am not sure we can be (or need to be) all that precise here. Scripture does not give us a great deal of data, but it also gives us no reason to worry. It seems at least in the case of very young adopted children, the Spirit would begin working immediately. The child has been brought into a covenant family. The child now has a right to baptism. He is "engaged" to the Lord, and so the Spirit, as the Divine Matchmaker, begins preparing the child to "marry" Christ in baptism by working faith in him.

This should not strike us as odd. There are several places in the gospels where the faith of a believing parent obtains some great blessing for a child or even a servant (cf. Mt. 8:5–13; 15:21–28). In other words, children, including non-biological children like servants or adoptees, are beneficiaries of their guardian's faith. They are beneficiaries of the faith community into which they have been grafted. There is good warrant for believing that the new bonds that tie together the adopted child and his believing parents are consecrated by God, so that faith spreads as the Spirit flows out from the hearts of the parents in love and nurture toward the child (cf. Jn. 7:38). There is no reason why an adopted newborn should not begin exercising paedofaith from the moment his new family takes him in and holds him, touches him, and speaks to him.

This is not an unusual position in Reformed theology. For example, Mark Horne's research uncovered a General Assembly report written by Charles Hodge in 1843 in which the question of the baptism of orphans came up. The Christian orphanage asked Presbytery for advice. Should very young children from heathen backgrounds be baptized if they are committed to the care of the mission? The presbyters answered in the affirmative, arguing that if there was a reasonable expectation that the children would receive a Christian education, they were fit to receive baptism. Discipleship is the issue (Mt. 28:18–20). If they are going to be discipled, they are under the care and covering of a believing covenantal institution.[24]

---

24. The report may be accessed at http://www.hornes.org/theologia/content/charles_hodge/baptism_of_orphans.htm.

# four

## _infants dying in infancy_

The question of infants dying in infancy is an interesting and important test case for how all of this works out in the life of the church. It also touches on one of the most pastorally sensitive issues we face. Most theologians do not want to argue that _all_ dying infants are lost to perdition, even though God is not intrinsically obligated to save any of them because they are fallen in Adam. The mainstream Calvinist tradition admits such children are capable of receiving salvation, and in fact the tradition usually argues that covenant infants who are taken from this life before maturing are undoubtedly saved (Scotch Confession, chapter sixteen; Synod of Dordt 1.16).

Ultimately, the question here is simple: what has God promised to our children? The biblical answer is clear: He has promised them Himself. He has promised to give Himself to them in the covenant to be their God (Gen. 17:7). He has promised them His righteousness (Ps. 103:17). He has promised them His Spirit (Isa. 59:21). He has promised them holiness (1 Cor. 7:14). He promised to make them Christ's disciples (Mt. 28:18–20). He has promised them forgiveness (Acts 2:38–39). All taken together, it adds up to a promise of salvation (Acts 16:31).

Thus, the claim that covenant infants dying in infancy are saved
has strong plausibility, even at first glance. Yet granting the possibility
of infant salvation, we have to ask *how* infants are saved. Are they saved
by faith or apart from faith? Some say no, they cannot be saved through
faith because infant faith bends the Reformed definition of faith (knowledge, assent, trust) out of shape. There is no such thing as paedofaith.

But the alternatives are to say that a) infants are saved by Christ
apart from faith, which twists the biblical doctrine of *sola fide* to the
breaking point and fragments the unity of salvation in Christ; or
b) infants are saved without faith because they are morally innocent,
thus denying the biblical and historic doctrine of original sin in a Pela-
gian fashion. Either one of these alternatives argues for something not
taught anywhere in Scripture, namely, salvation apart from faith, which
is to say, apart from a relationship with the Triune God. Also, either one
of these alternatives leaves us with at least two ways of salvation—
salvation *by* faith for those who have cognitive abilities, and salvation
*apart from* faith for those who lack such abilities. However we may seek
to escape the horns of the dilemma, it seems that denying paedofaith
actually creates more problems than it solves.

I admit that this issue has not reached full resolution in the history of
theology, and far be it from me to suppose I can solve it here to everyone's satisfaction. The Westminster divines acknowledged the thorni-
ness of this issue in WCF 10.3. This section of the Confession walks a
fine line between several different positions without really excluding or
insisting upon any of them. It is rather open-ended, allowing Presbyterian theologians liberty to come to their own convictions within certain
boundaries. Whatever we say about infant salvation, it must not become
a new test of orthodoxy. We should be charitable toward those who see
things differently.

Nevertheless, we should pursue the issue as far as we can. Let's
look more closely at this section of the Confession. WCF 10.3 asserts that
elect infants dying in infancy are saved. This is a tautology, of course,
since any elect person who dies at any age will inevitably be
saved (cf. WCF 3). The Confession stubbornly refuses to identify who
these saved infants are. One could believe that all, some, or none of
those infants who die in infancy are elect. One could tie this infant sal-

vation directly to the covenant or not depending on other considerations.

The Confession then goes on to say that these elect infants who are saved are saved by Christ through the Spirit. Thus, infant salvation is *not* an exception to *solus Christus* or *sola gratia*. Even covenant infants are sinners in need of remission and regeneration. The means used to bring about this salvation, however, are not specified since Christ works "when and where and how He pleaseth." These infants who are saved are regenerated, but the Confession is careful to *not* say that they have faith. So the *possibility* that infant salvation is an exception to *sola fide* is left open by the Confession, at least theoretically.[1]

While I want to acknowledge the difficulty of the problem here, I think admitting the possibility—or better, the normativity—of infant faith, in accord with the evidence marshaled above, goes a long way toward a suitable solution. Relying on the biblical data that suggest infant faith is normative for the children of believers, we can say with confidence that all covenant infants dying in infancy are saved.

In other words, understanding paedofaith can help us deal with an immensely difficult pastoral problem. While infant mortality rates are not what they once were (thanks be to God), it is still a common and deeply painful experience to lose a child in infancy (including miscarriages). I believe there is strong biblical warrant for telling believing parents that they will see their lost child again. David certainly had this hope (cf. 2 Sam. 12:22–23). The same divine promise that grounds the child's right to baptism ensures his salvation. The same declaration of Jesus that includes the child in the kingdom on earth includes him in glory in heaven. In other words, it makes good sense to tie together the covenant promises, paedofaith, and infant salvation into a package.

Paedofaith gives us a theologically compelling and pastorally comforting account of infant salvation, more so than many accounts that

---

1. All this is to say that the question of infant faith is really outside the scope of the Confession. The Westminster divines did not pronounce on it one way or another, so it is an extra-confessional issue. At the very least, 10.3 holds out the possibility of infant regeneration, which means infant faith must be at least possible—unless we want to say there are regenerate unbelievers!

have been offered in the past.[2] Why should paedofaith be regarded as an impossibility? Is it psychologically impossible for the infant? How do we know? Is it too hard for God to give infants the gift of faith? Surely not! If God can save infants, He can give them faith. To deny *sola fide* by making infants dying in infancy an exception seems entirely unnecessary. That approach not only overlooks the paedofaith passages we have examined, it also inserts major qualifiers into other texts that ascribe salvation to the instrumentality of faith alone.

Moreover, divorcing the salvation of infants dying in infancy from faith runs the risk of severing their salvation from the gospel itself. While the Westminster Confession insists saved infants are redeemed by Christ and the Spirit, if we do not include paedofaith in the picture, we have no way of linking these infants with Christ. But this is not the biblical way of salvation. As Calvin pointed out, all that Christ has accomplished is of no value for us until we are united to Him by faith. Indeed, faith is the only way we can be bonded to Christ and receive His benefits. If paedofaith seems absurd, salvation apart from faith is even more problematic! Some theologians have denied paedofaith and still insisted that (at the very least) covenant infants dying in infancy are saved, but this creates a virtually unbearable tension in one's theological system.

While our standard accounts of faith are fine as far as they go, as already noted, they are too cognitive to be applicable to infants. The triad of knowledge, assent, and trust works well in the case of adults, but seems unable to account for passages like Psalm 22:9–10 and Matthew 18:5. Once again, I would suggest that knowledge, assent, and trust comprise *mature* faith, while *infant* faith is simply an age-appropriate expression of personal trust. Factual knowledge and assent will be added in later, but in the meantime nothing keeps the child from having a trusting relationship with God any more than the child is prevented from developing a relationship with his parents prior to attaining rational and verbal abilities.[3]

---

2. See the bibliographic essay on page 153.

3. To reiterate, paedofaith does not require a wholesale redefinition of faith in the Reformed tradition, but it does require us to make some nuances and distinctions. Peter Leithart provides a fascinating account of the rationality of infant faith in his short article "Do Baptists Talk to Their Babies?" available at http://www.biblicalhorizons.com/rr/rr047.htm. Asking "When can a developing

The child has knowledge—personal, relational knowledge—of God in the same way he has personal, relational knowledge of his mother. This knowledge is fully sufficient to serve as a means of salvation.[4]

---

infant begin to exercise faith?" is part and parcel of the larger question "When can an *in utero* child begin to have personal relationships?" When we ask "Can babies have faith?" we are really asking "Can babies have relations with other persons? Is it possible to communicate with a baby?" No matter how much rationalists in the Church may deny the possibility of infant faith, at this point, common sense and parental practice show otherwise. Parents talk to their infants and communicate with them in verbal and non-verbal ways long before the child develops mental faculties. The child is capable of some kind of response, however inarticulate. If parents can relate to the baby this way, why not God, who is infinitely closer to the child? Furthermore, insofar as personhood is a function of relationality ("to be a person is to be in relation"), it would seem that to deny that the infant in the womb can have relationships is to view it as less than a person—an observation that has chilling implications, as we've already indicated. Some Anabaptists moved in just this direction when they said that baptizing a baby was no different than dipping a cat or stick in the water, because they are all lacking in rationality.

This account of "personhood as relationship" is rooted in the Trinity. For a Reformed exploration of the topic, see another Leithart article, "Trinitarian Anthropology: Toward a Trinitarian Recasting of Reformed Theology" in *The Auburn Avenue Theology: Pros and Cons*, edited by Calvin Beisner (Fort Lauderdale: Knox Theological Seminary, 2004), 58ff. Michael Polanyi's personalist epistemology is also relevant here since Polanyi shows that knowledge and articulation are not always identical. Indeed, we know more than we can say in almost every area of life. For a Reformed introduction to relational knowledge, see Esther Lightcap Meek, *Longing to Know: The Philosophy of Knowledge for Ordinary People* (Grand Rapids: Brazos, 2003).

4. Obviously, then, I would argue that *all covenant infants dying in infancy* are saved. I am happily agnostic about non-covenant infants who perish in infancy, but Scripture gives no solid basis for hoping they are saved apart from a general appeal to God's mercy. God may save them if He graciously chooses to, or He may justly leave them to perish under the curse of Adam's sin.

There is a deep irony in the way we deal with the children of believers in much of the contemporary Reformed world. For children of believers who live, their baptisms are regarded as latent (at best) until they "come of age." Reformed and Presbyterian folks usually know better than to speak of an "age of accountability," but they function with one nonetheless, though the actual age at which a child's profession may be regarded as mature enough to secure access to heaven (and/or to the Lord's Table) may vary widely, from two years old up to twenty. However, when a covenant child dies in infancy (or even youth), many (though admittedly not all) of these same people regard the child as saved because of God's covenant promises. The deceased child's funeral proceeds according to

Lest this seem too strange, remember that even in the womb God is infinitely closer to the child than the parents. God is never denied access to His creatures, even those who are not yet fully developed mentally and emotionally.[5] The promise is for us and for our children—including our stillborn children, our miscarried children, our children who die in their youth, and our mentally impaired children (Acts 2:39; cf. Ps. 103:17; Isa. 59:21; 65:23). God deals with us trans-generationally. He has bound us together with our children in a common covenant bond of faith and life. Let no man separate what God has joined together—Christian parents and their offspring. The gospel is for us and for our children, and parents who trust God's promises will not be disappointed.

---

this view, and the covenant promises are offered as comfort to the grieving parents. It is very odd, to say the least, that those promises are regarded as insufficient for the child's salvation (and communing membership) in the present should he live, but suddenly become so should he die. This is theologically schizophrenic. It makes our claim to salvation for the child who died in youth seem shallow and sentimental. Covenant promises are made effective through faith, not death. As R. C. Sproul Jr. once pointed out, we must be leery of all versions of "justification by youth alone."

5. Thus, Jesus could heal a deaf-mute (Mk. 7:31–37). Indeed, God even has access to the dead (cf. Jn. 11:38ff). What God can work in us is not at all dependent on our native or inherent abilities. If God can work life in a human corpse, He can work faith in living infants. Nothing is too hard for God.

five

# the universality of paedofaith
## in covenant children:
### exceptions and qualifications

Thus far, we have argued for the normativity of paedofaith in covenant children. From the point of conception onward, covenant children are sinners, indeed, but sinners who have a trusting relationship with their heavenly Father. God's promises are theirs, and their hope is in the Lord. God's Spirit is at work in them, and they are already distinguished from the children of the world. They have a covenant relationship of mutual faithfulness: their faith is in God, and He is a faithful Father to them.

But does this apply to *every* covenant child, head for head? Are there any exceptions? How universal is paedofaith amongst baptized infants? What about *my* child?

This is a tricky question. In terms of a child's objective status, he's either in the covenant (or on the way into the covenant) or outside the covenant. If he's baptized, or has a right to baptism, the covenant promises belong to him. If he is not part of a believing family, he has no share in the covenant blessings, promises, or privileges (and should not be baptized).

I conclude there is biblical warrant for saying that *every child who has a legitimate right to baptism, or who has been legitimately baptized, may be regarded as a believer until and unless proven otherwise.*[1] The evidence offered thus far clinches this conclusion. The children of believers are believers themselves. They share in the faith of their parents, not by some natural transmission of this virtue, but because of the trans-generational promise of God's covenant and the work of the Spirit.

Clearly, covenant children are not *against* the kingdom of God. Jesus included them in His kingdom, after all (Mt. 18:3, 6; 19:14). Nor are they *neutral* toward the kingdom, for ethical neutrality is impossible in God's universe (Mt. 12:30). The only alternative left is what we have already seen, again and again: covenant children belong to Jesus, and live and move and have their being within the circle of His kingdom blessings. This is normative for the children of believers, for they are part of the believing community.

But this leaves us with a further issue. Some children are baptized when they really should not have been.[2] Perhaps the church is apostate and only practices a hollow shell of baptism with no living faith in the community. In such a case, infant baptism can hardly be said to graft the child into the believing community because the community itself is unfaithful. The baptism may be valid, but unbelief nullifies the gracious side of baptismal efficacy. Only intensified judgment is left. The child's baptism puts him under the covenant, but almost surely as a covenant-breaker. He violates the covenant the moment he enters it.

---

1. Do not confuse *legitimacy* with *validity* here. Many people receive valid baptisms (baptisms done according to proper, Triune form) that are illegitimate (because they should not have been baptized according to biblical standards of covenant entrance). But even illegitimate baptisms are still baptisms.

2. Gunton, in "Baptism and the Christian Community," does a fine job dealing with whom (including whose children) should be baptized. The Church's indiscriminant use of baptism, especially in Roman Catholic and mainline Protestant churches, has done much to bring shame on the name of Christ in the world. The children of "Christmas and Easter Christians" (those who only attend church twice a year or so) should not be baptized. We must "fence the font," so to speak. We should only baptize children when there is at least one believing sponsor/parent, and there is a reasonable expectation that the child will receive some measure of covenant nurture in the faith.

In other cases, the parents are apostate. The church should not have baptized their children because the parents gave no evidence of a vital relationship with Christ. The child has no real hope of receiving Christian nurture, and if church discipline had been applied more vigilantly, the child would not have been baptized at all. The breakdown in church discipline leads to an irregularity in the life of the church. Again, we have covenant children who are in an anomalous situation.

In cases like these, the sacrament of baptism is abused and the presence of paedofaith is doubtful at best. Paedofaith only makes sense when the child is made part of *believing* ecclesial and familial communities. Within the network of these faith communities, enmeshed in faith-filled relationships, the child's faith will receive constant nurture and encouragement.[3] Without such external sustenance, even if the child has faith in infancy, it is unlikely the faith will persevere. Apostasy (whether immediate or not) is more likely than perseverance.[4] The infant has faith only

---

3. Mark 2:1–12 is a good example of the importance of "communal faith." Several men bring a paralytic to Jesus for healing. When Jesus saw *their* faith, the man received forgiveness and (just afterward) healing. Certainly the paralytic had faith, but the emphasis is on the *faith community* of which he is a part. His friends believed the gospel on his behalf, and therefore brought him to Jesus. He was a beneficiary of corporate faith.

Believing parents are doing the same thing when they bring their babies for baptism. They believe the gospel for the sake of their children. There are several biblical accounts of Jesus acting on behalf of a child because the parent exercised faith. In some of these cases, the child may not have had faith (e.g., the child was already dead or was demon-possessed), but it is a safe assumption that in each of these cases the child came to share his or her parent's faith afterwards. See Matthew 8:5–13; 9:18–26; 15:21–29, etc. Medieval theologians Anselm and Bernard based their view of infant salvation on this type of corporate faith: the faith of the parents (or the Church) interposes on behalf of the child.

When considering the faith of our children, it is fair to start with the corporate faith of the church body of which they are a part. We are not isolated atoms, but molecules, interrelated and interdependent. Our children are grafted into the living, faith-filled, Spirit-created organism of the new Israel. This corporate faith ensures their individual faith. When you have authentic corporate faith, you get individual faith thrown in as well. The individual and the corporate interpenetrate one another. The child's faith will become more and more individualized as he matures, but at the same time it will be more and more closely intertwined with the community's life of faith.

4. The parable of the soils gives us a helpful typology of unbelief within the covenant (Mt. 13:1–9, 18–23). While the seed in the parable is the word of God, not

when considered as a member of the *people of faith*, the community knit-
ted together by a web of faith-filled relationships. Baptism is rightly
used only in a context of communal faith.[5]

We should note, then, the positive outworking of this: in a healthy
church there is *no reason* to doubt the paedofaith of *all* the children who
are brought for baptism. Given that most Reformed and Presbyterian
churches are fairly careful about baptizing only the children of believing
sponsors, we may speak of a kind of universality of infant faith in our
circles. When we turn to deal with other, less faithful communions, our
degree of certainty wanes, to be sure. The lack of corporate faith makes
the presence of individual faith tenuous at best. However, this lack of
certainty is *not* because paedofaith is not actually the norm; rather it is
due to the abnormality of Christian churches and families that do not
adequately believe and practice the gospel.[6]

---

baptism per se, it is still relevant since the same issues are involved. Baptism is
simply a sacramental application of the word.

According to the parable, some may have the seed of the gospel snatched
away by Satan almost immediately. I would think this would be very applicable
in the case of infants baptized in unbelieving, corrupt families and churches.
Individual and communal unbelief blocks the efficacy of the sacrament from the
outset, so the offer of new life and forgiveness bound up in baptism is refused.
The objective efficacy of baptism is still in force, but subjectively the blessings of
baptism are never received. At baptism, the child simply becomes a faithless
covenant member and falls under the covenant's negative sanctions. In other
cases, the gospel seed may be received with joy, but only for a time. Eventually,
the child's faith withers, resulting in apostasy. Of course, if the child is elected
unto eternal salvation, then he will respond with a persevering faith and "improve" his baptism through the whole course of his life.

5. This gets us back to an intra-Protestant debate that has raged since the
time of the Reformation. Assuming baptismal questions are used in the sacramental celebration, to whom should those vows be addressed? The Lutherans
address the questions directly to the child, indicating that the child is baptized
primarily in consideration of his own faith. The Reformed have traditionally
addressed the questions to the sponsors/parents, indicating that the baptism is
grounded in parental (and communal) trust in the covenant promises. Who is
right? Both are, of course. Paedobaptism stands at the nexus of commu-
nal/parental faith, in which the strong believe the gospel on behalf of the weak,
and individual paedofaith, in which the child knows God as Father by virtue of
his own faith. The faith of the church, the parents, and the child all play a role.

6. For a similar conclusion, see Hoffmann, 92–93 and Gunton, 104ff.

The normalcy of baby faith is assumed in every passage we looked at earlier in our study. Infant faith is simply a corollary of our broader theology of covenant children. Consider again David's claim in Psalm 22:9–10. If I am a Christian parent, there is no reason why I cannot place these words on the lips of my own children. Indeed, they should learn this Psalm and take it to heart as a way of expressing their own life in the covenant.

How do we know the paedofaith of Psalm 22 can be universalized and personalized to covenant infants in this way? David is not basing his claim to infant trust on remembered experience (since no one remembers infancy), but on the covenant promises as such. Thus, we can be sure that infant faith is a common possession of covenant children. David *knew* he trusted in God because, for a child of the promise, a relationship with God is always already there—and that relationship consists in mutual faithfulness.

The promise that God is a God to our children gives them *at least* an initial gift of faith which may then be cultivated and brought to maturity through parental and ecclesial nurture (or may whither and die if not so nurtured). David's knowledge of the faith that he had as an infant was derived from more universal covenantal principles that would be applicable to any child in any believing household. If David could know these things about his pre-conscious experience, there's no reason other cases shouldn't be treated in the same way, drawing the same inferences from the same premises. Thus, paedofaith is the norm in the covenant community. We trust God to be a God to our children because of His covenant promises; at the same time, we may be sure that our children trust God themselves. This faith may be shaped somewhat differently by our respective roles and positions in the covenant, but we may be sure we share together in the life of the covenant of faith.

six

## *paedofaith in protestant history*

Many in the Protestant tradition have acknowledged at least the possibility (if not the normativity) of paedofaith. It is not my purpose here to give a full history, but only to cite a few pieces of relevant evidence and make a tentative assessment. This survey should demonstrate that paedofaith is well within the parameters of historic Protestant orthodoxy, especially the classical Lutheran and Reformed traditions. It is also important for us to see how the doctrine of paedofaith was lost. The rise of revivalism established a conversionist paradigm at the expense of a covenant nurture paradigm and emphasized dramatic one-time experiences over against steady, faithful participation in the ordinary means of grace. These changes were not favorable to covenant children, as the focus came to be more and more on what our children might become, as opposed to what they already are.

## Martin Luther

At the time of the Reformation, paedobaptism was typically grounded
either in the corporate faith of the Church or the expectation of future
faith on the part of the child. Martin Luther countered these views in
1525, arguing that infant baptism should be grounded in the infant's
own faith. This was part of his project of personalizing the gospel. If
infants do not have faith, he said, they should not be baptized. Baptism
belongs to believers and them only.

> Now if we could not give any better answer to this question and
> prove that young children themselves believe and have a faith of
> their own, then it is my faithful counsel and judgment that we
> should with immediate effect desist from this practice, yes, the
> sooner the better, and baptize not a single child more, lest we
> should mock and blaspheme the praiseworthy majesty of God
> with such unfounded tomfoolery and trickery . . . Faith must be
> present before or rather in baptism, otherwise the child is not free
> of the devil and sin.[1]

Of course, Luther was not willing to give up the practice of baptizing
infants. He believed that infants had faith, for there was no other way
for them to enter into Christ's kingdom and salvation. Luther argued
strongly against the Bohemian Brethren and others who grounded infant baptism in the *future* faith of the child. Infant faith has continued to
be a part of the Lutheran theological tradition and has at times helped
protect Lutheranism from the encroachments of rationalism.[2]

---

1. Quoted in Hoffmann, 82.
2. Many sources could be cited. See, e.g., John Theodore Mueller, *Christian
Dogmatics* (St. Louis: Concordia Publishing House, 1934), 498, 502; David Scaer,
*Baptism: Confessional Lutheran Dogmatics, Vol. 9* (St. Louis: The Luther Academy,
1999), chapter ten; and A. Andrew Das, *Baptized into God's Family: The Doctrine of
Infant Baptism Today* (Milwaukee: Northwestern Publishing House, 1991), chapters three and four. Lutherans typically argue that infant faith is not "latent" or
"potential" but an actual faith that receives and grasps the promises offered in
baptism. Infants are baptized because of their own faith; Lutheran baptismal
liturgies accordingly address the pre-baptismal questions to the child (though of
course a sponsor still answers). Many Lutheran accounts of infant faith differ
from Reformed accounts in that Lutherans view baptism as actually creating
faith in the heart of the child, whereas the Reformed are more likely to view faith
as already present in an incipient form before baptism, so that in baptism the

## John Calvin

John Calvin's position was very similar to Luther's. Calvin spoke of baptized infants as having a "seed" of faith. This protofaith would eventually mature into fully-actualized adult faith in the case of the elect. However, the seed illustration does *not* mean that faith in the child is only a matter of potentiality. As Calvin unfolds the way he understands God's work in the infant, it becomes clear that he believes infant faith and adult faith stand in a continuum. Infant faith is not merely a dormant virtue, awaiting some later development to awaken it. While Calvin struggles to describe infant faith, he has no qualms about robustly affirming that God can and does work faith in infants by His Spirit. He does not view infant faith as something rare or strange. Indeed, he gives it a kind of normativity, and connects it with the sacrament of initiation. Infant faith is a significant component of Calvin's theology.

Calvin argues that infants can experience the grace of regeneration in Christ in *Institutes* 4.16.17 and 4.16.18. In the next section, he responds to the (Anabaptist) argument that infants should not be baptized because they cannot understand preaching.

> Many He certainly has called and endued with the true knowledge of Himself by internal means, by the illumination of the Spirit, without the intervention of preaching. But since they deem it very absurd to attribute any knowledge of God to infants, whom Moses makes void of the knowledge of good and evil, let them tell me where the danger lies if they are said now to receive some part of that grace, of which they are to have the full measure shortly after. For if fullness of life consists in the perfect knowledge of God, since some of those whom death hurries away in the first moments of infancy pass into life eternal, they are certainly admitted to behold the immediate presence of God. Those therefore whom the Lord is to illumine with the full brightness of His light, why may He not, if He so pleases, irradiate at present with some small beam, especially if He does not remove their ignorance before He delivers them from the prison of the flesh? I would not rashly affirm that they are endued with the same faith which we experience in ourselves or have any knowledge at all resembling faith, (this I

---

child's faith receives Christ as he is offered and his faith is thereby strengthened and confirmed.

would rather leave undecided); but I would somewhat curb the
stolid arrogance of those men who, as with inflated cheeks affirm
or deny whatever suits them.

Several points here are worthy of close attention. Calvin says infants can
receive in infancy some small measure of the fuller grace they will receive later in life. They do not have the "same faith" as adult believers
because their faith does not include the same kind of knowledge. But
they are still capable of receiving inner operations of grace, presumably
a kind of incipient faith. This is especially important in the case of infants dying in infancy: Calvin does not want to make their salvation an
exception to *sola fide*. But he indicates other infants who grow to maturity may have faith as well. Nothing indicates that Calvin thought of
infant faith as a rarity; indeed, he seems to regard all covenant infants as
subjects of the Spirit's work.

Calvin acknowledges that paedofaith is different from adult faith,
but he is content to leave the nature of such faith undetermined, beyond
the obvious admission that infants do not have knowledge like we do as
adults. However difficult it might be to conceive of faith in infants, only
"stolid arrogance" (that is, stubborn rationalism) would lead someone
to deny the possibility of infant believers. Infants are capable of a "small
beam" of grace, which may give way to full light later on in life. This
illumination even in infancy is God's gift and can justly be called
"faith."

In 4.16.20, Calvin furthers the point. Baptism (like circumcision) is a
sacrament of faith and repentance; thus, only repentant believers should
receive it. Any objection to paedobaptism is also an objection to paedo-
circumcision, but everyone agrees that infants were to be circumcised in
old covenant Israel.

> For although infants, at the very moment they were circumcised,
> did not comprehend with their understanding what the sign
> meant, they were truly circumcised to the mortification of their
> corrupt and defiled nature, a mortification that they would after-
> ward practice in mature years. To sum up, this objection can be
> solved without difficulty: infants are baptized into future repen-
> tance and faith, and even though these have not yet been formed

in them, the seed of both lies within them by the secret working of the Spirit.

Calvin says infants could not grasp the meaning of the sign with their understanding, but this does not preclude their grasping it by faith. Here again, Calvin distinguishes adult faith and repentance from the infantile form of these virtues, which he calls their "seed." Faith and repentance are present in infants in an inchoate, seminal form. In time, they will come to fuller and more active expression. Calvin clearly views infant faith as organically related to adult faith. A covenant child would not need to have a "conversion experience" in order to become a believer; he simply needs to grow in the faith he possessed even as an infant. Calvin was no revivalist.

Because of the secret working of God's Spirit, we can speak of covenant infants as already trusting in God. Calvin affirms paedofaith, though this does not preclude distinguishing paedofaith from adult faith. He admits that God's renewing work in infants is incomprehensible to us (cf. 4.16.21). (Of course, his work in adults is incomprehensible as well!) Calvin acknowledges paedofaith is a mystery. The Spirit's work is not outwardly traceable in infants in the same way as adults (which means we discern its presence not through examining external evidence but through trusting the covenant promises).

Interestingly, in 4.16.20, he locates the difference between infant and adult faith not so much in knowledge as in the *practice* of mortification. But infant faith must be in some kind of direct continuity with the faith that comes later, or else his "seed" imagery wouldn't work. The seed of faith means the faith present in the child will blossom into fruitful, mature faith later on, but even the "seed" of faith is faith, albeit immature faith. Seed faith is essentially invisible to us, but contains within itself covenant life. Mortification begins, in principle, when the covenant sign is first received by seed faith; the "actualization" of faith in later life is coordinated with the actual practice of mortification. This seems to be Calvin's paradigm. As a covenant child grows up he moves from faith to ever greater and more mature faith (rather than moving from rank unbelief to faith, as in conversionist paradigms).

While Calvin affirms that infants may be illuminated with a kind of faith which will later grow into practicing faithfulness, his discussion of infant faith is not without flaws. Calvin's view of faith is sometimes overly cognitive and not fully relational. Calvin's affirmation of seed faith in covenant infants could have been bolstered by a fuller discussion of actual instances of child piety recorded in Scripture, though Calvin generally fails to bring these texts (e.g., Ps. 22:9–10) into the discussion. Nevertheless, Calvin still affirms the basic point: God can work graciously even in children still in the womb. The light He gives them and the seed He plants within them is the beginning of a life of faith. The mortification of the flesh begins the moment the sign of the covenant is received because the infant already has faith after a fashion and thus receives the sign rightly. Because our covenant children are believers, we should nurture them accordingly.

Calvin grounds infant baptism primarily in his doctrine of the covenant, yet he sees infant faith as a subsidiary argument for the practice and a corollary of the covenant membership of infants. Calvin's position is biblical, nuanced, and pastoral. Other notable continental Reformed theologians such as Ulrich Zwingli, Heinrich Bullinger, Theodore Beza, Peter Martyr Vermigli, Peter Jurieu, Jerome Zanchius, Zacharius Ursinus, Johann Alsted, Wolfgang Musculus, Antonius Walaeus, and Francis Junius basically shared Calvin's view of infant seed faith.[3] The Calvinian tradi-

---

3. These theologians varied as to how robust they were in their assertions about infant faith, some going further than Calvin, others slightly weakening Calvin's view. Some might argue Beza does not belong in this list because of his firm denial of infant faith in his debate with the Lutheran Jacob Andrae at Montbeliard. See Jill Raitt, "*Probably* They Are God's Children" in *Humanism and Reformed: The Church in Europe, England, and Scotland, 1400–1643*, edited by James Kirk (Oxford: Blackwell, 1991), 151ff. However, in some places Beza does in fact affirm a seed of faith in infants, even if he means less by this than Calvin did.

A handy survey of some continental Reformed options regarding paedo-baptism and paedofaith may be found in *Redemptive History and Biblical Interpretation: The Shorter Writings of Geerhardus Vos*, edited by Richard B. Gaffin (Phillipsburg, NJ: Presbyterian and Reformed, 1980), 263ff.

See also Hughes Oliphant Old, *The Shaping of the Reformed Baptismal Rite in the Sixteenth Century* (Grand Rapids: Eerdmans, 1992), 133ff. Old argues the Reformers grounded paedobaptism, at least in part, in the fact that "the Holy Spirit is at work with children of believers from the very beginning of life. Christ begins His work of redemption in their hearts even before they have the power of reason. . . . The Reformers were quite willing to admit the existence of faith in

tion was generally faithful to its master on this point well into the seventeenth century.

### Francis Turretin

Francis Turretin's scholastic work *Institutes of Elenctic Theology* illustrates the manner in which the later Reformed orthodox divines handled the question of infant faith. By the late 1600s, Reformed theology had come into its own as a system polemically distinct from Lutheranism and other varieties of Protestant faith. While Turretin sought to uphold Calvin's basic position on paedofaith, he brought in some new distinctions and qualifications that would slowly weaken the church's resolve to uphold a doctrine of infant faith in the face of a rising rationalism in Western philosophy. Infant faith (admittedly, a deep mystery) became the victim of increasing precision in systematic theology.

In *Institutes* 15.14, Turretin says that the Reformed steer a middle course between the Anabaptists' denial of infant faith and the Lutheran view of actualized faith in infants. Turretin refuses to grant *actual* faith to infants because faith relies instrumentally upon reason and knowledge, which infants do not possess. The intellect, according to Turretin, must be active in order to exercise assent and trust, since these functions require that the object of faith be expressly known. The use of reason (and thus the grasp of propositions) seems to be the fundamental difference between infant faith and actual faith. Turretin does not really engage Lutheran arguments for actual faith in infants. Nor does he explain why faith depends on cognition; he simply assumes it.

---

children before the development of understanding. . . . The simple childlike trust which children have before the age of reason is precisely the kind of faith which Jesus held up as exemplary to His disciples. . . . Before children are able to make a reasonable judgment or even a conscious decision, they can have faith as a gift from God. This faith is a trusting and loving inclination toward God. Faith is something deeper than either the reason or the will. It is something which, by the grace of God, the Spirit plants within us. Both obedience and understanding proceed from it." The Reformers did not arrive at this doctrine of *fides infantium* simply for polemical purposes (that is, to prop up the practice of paedobaptism). Rather, it grew organically out of their understanding of faith as a divine gift. The paedobaptism/paedofaith complex was a logical corollary of *sola gratia*.

Unfortunately, Turretin does little biblical exegesis. He suggests
that the children in Matthew 18:6 are not helpful in discussing infant
faith because the children are old enough to be "called" and "offended"—that is to say, they are capable of receiving instruction. But
Turretin does not interact with any of the key Old Testament texts we
examined above other than a brief reference to Psalm 8:2. Further, while
he grants that cases like Jeremiah and John the Baptist indicate children
can receive the sanctifying work of the Holy Spirit in infancy, he rejects
the notion that they *actually* believed in the way adults do. In the case of
John the Baptist, this is raises a key question: How is his faith-leap in the
womb consistent with the *denial* of active faith in infants? How active
did John need to be to have active (or actual) faith? The problem is not
so much that Turretin wants to distinguish infant faith from adult faith
(since there are obvious differences). Rather, the issue is that Turretin
creates the impression that infant faith is an oddity, rather than normative in some way. He overemphasizes the role of the intellect and un-
deremphasizes relationality, calling into question the continuity
between infant faith and adult faith.

In the case of infants, baptism is an objective seal of the covenant
and thus efficacious; but infants do not actually receive the benefits of
baptism in full since these "cannot be known or received by faith" in the
case of infants. While infants are recipients of the covenant promises so
that the blessings of the covenant (including remission and sanctification) pertain to them, their holiness is more external and federal than
real and actual. Turretin appears to accept an anthropological dualism
here, as he does not explain how a person can be holy in a merely exter-
nalized way without that holiness impinging upon his internal identity.
The sociological and the Spiritual are not so easily separated. Further,
this limitation of infant baptism's efficacy is in tension with other statements Turretin makes about baptism elsewhere. It has the tendency of
creating some measure of doubt about the status of our covenant children, even though on the whole Turretin clearly wants to affirm that
covenant children belong to God and to His people.

Turretin's "seed faith" is not identical to Calvin's. Turretin wants it
both ways: he wants to be able to acknowledge the infant already possesses some kind of covenant life (per Calvin), yet he also wants to

maintain a more scholastic, intellectualized definition of faith. Turretin, then, is something of a bridge between Calvin and Reformed scholasticism, but as a result, he wavers quite a bit on the question of infant faith. The flaw in Turretin's discussion here is his lack of explanation of what he means by "the seed or root of faith" which he is willing to ascribe to covenant infants, even as he denies the presence of actual faith in infants. He uses Calvin's form of words ("seed faith") but has significantly attenuated his position. If infants cannot have faith, how can they have its seed? What is this "seed" and how does it differ from actual faith? Is it organically related to adult faith (as in Calvin)? If faith is more a matter of intellectual knowledge than relational trust, as Turretin suggests, how can infants possess faith *at all*, even in seminal form? There is some tension between what Turretin wants to affirm about infants and the way he wants to define faith.

If all Turretin means by these distinctions is that infant faith is more passive than active, fair enough; but at some points he seems to imply that infant faith is altogether latent. Again, latent faith would be hard to fit with David's more active description of trust in the Psalter and with John the Baptist's active leap in Elizabeth's womb. In fact, the active/passive faith distinction seems rather unhelpful in the end. Again, Turretin lacks the necessary relational categories to make sense of paedofaith. He preserves the doctrine of infant faith, but only with some awkwardness.

The claim that infant faith is "inactive" also stands in tension with the way Turretin describes the Spirit's work in our children. If infants have the Spirit, and the Spirit "cannot be inactive" as Turretin admits, why can't these infants have a kind of Spirit-actualized faith in some sense? The most Turretin will say is that this "seed" is "potential" faith, a faith that will grow into being at a later time. This "potential" faith, in Turretin's view, is simply the presence of the Holy Spirit, "who already works in infants according to their measure in a wonderful and unspeakable way" and will bring forth faith in the child at a more mature age, when he receives instruction.

Again, it is not all clear how this view squares with the claims of David in Psalm 22:9–10 which do not distinguish a *seed* of trust from an *act* of trust. David was not speaking merely of his potential to become an actual believer later on in life. Nor is it clear how all this squares with Turretin's own point that the Spirit works in our children "motions and inclinations suited to their age." If the Spirit is actually at work in our infants, why must we insist that their faith is merely a matter of potential? The case against non-cognitive-but-actual-and-relational-infant-faith has not been made.

None of this denies the value of Turretin's discussion. He says many good things about the reality of infant faith, the work of the Spirit, the significance of infant baptism, and the covenantal status of our children. The good certainly outweighs the bad. Revivalists and conversionists will find little to aid their approach in Turretin. Those who want to pursue a course of covenant nurture will be greatly encouraged by Turretin's comments. He definitely stands in the paedofaith tradition.

Nevertheless, Turretin's nuances do little to further the discussion beyond Calvin and in some ways take a step backwards. Indeed, his fine nuances do more to confuse than clarify the issue. Turretin still believes in infant faith, but just barely. He comes close to qualifying it out of existence. In the rise of this sort of scholasticism, however helpful it might otherwise be, the way is being prepared for a significantly different view of covenant children.[4]

---

4. This is my suggestion in response to Turretin's dilemma. Instead of distinguishing "potential" faith from "actual" faith, we should distinguish the immature "seed" faith of infants from the more mature, knowledgeable faith of adults. "Potential" faith is far too ambiguous a category and seems to introduce too many extra-biblical qualifiers to paedofaith. "Latent" faith does not do justice to the biblical record. We need to do more to maintain the organic continuity of infant faith with adult faith.

As was often the case with the Reformed scholastic movement, here we see the scholastics desiring to provide a rigid answer to a question that Calvin left somewhat open-ended. Calvin was willing to leave the nature of infant faith undetermined. By saying less, he actually said more because he did not undermine the organic link between paedofaith and adult faith. The newly-introduced nuances in Turretin's day did at least as much to hinder the discussion as to help it. Plus, the scholastics often did very little detailed exegesis. Thus, their nuances are not clearly derived from the text of Scripture; therefore, they often feel artificial.

## The Puritans

The Puritans were not at all unified on sacramental issues, as the classic studies *The Covenant Sealed* by E. Brooks Holifield and *The Covenant Idea in New England Theology* by Peter DeJong demonstrate. Along with that diversity on the sacraments came diversity on the question of the status and condition of the covenant child. Within Puritanism, theologians and pastors took a wide array of positions, ranging from the view that infant faith is absurd, to saying infants could be regenerated but could not yet exercise faith, to claiming a robust paedofaith position. Of this last group, some said only elect infants dying in infancy received the gift of faith; others said some form of initial faith was common to *all* covenant children, though only the elect would grow to "actualize" that faith. Moreover, some theologians coordinated a doctrine of initial (infant) regeneration and later actual regeneration, with the seed of faith in infants and its mature form in older persons. Despite these various positions, we can identify a cadre of vigorous proponents of some view of paedofaith, including William Whittaker, Stephen Marshall, Thomas Blake, Josiah Church, Samuel Ward, Cornelius Burges, and John Davenant.

Let us look more closely at a few examples of Puritans who theologized positively about the possibility of paedofaith. John Cotton argued that "infants were capable of receiving faith from the Spirit and were therefore proper recipients of the seal of faith [baptism]." Cotton confessed that such faith could be recognized not by its effect, but only by the testimony of Scripture. In other words, children of believers were to be regarded as believers on the basis of the covenant promises until actual faith could be manifest. The covenant promises stood in place of a profession of faith until the children developed sufficient verbal abilities. The child cannot speak for himself, and so God speaks for him in His Word as a vicarious substitute.

Likewise, Thomas Hooker argued against the Baptists of his day that a "portion and provision" of grace must have been "appointed by God, and bestowed by God on some children." As Holifield explains Hooker's view, "If such infants were capable of grace, they also had a capacity for faith, which indeed, was proved by the fact that God 'must work faith in the hearts of all elect infants who die in their infancy,' faith being required for salvation." Hooker went so far as to argue that infants were "more capable" of grace than adults, and therefore more fit to receive the sacrament of baptism.[5]

Thomas Bedford, a student of Davenant, argued that baptismal regeneration extended to *all* baptized infants because infants are incapable of putting an obstacle in the way of its operation. No infant being brought for baptism is an unbeliever, according to Bedford. In his writings, Bedford relied on the work of Ward and Burges to make his case, arguing that baptism itself confers grace that will (or at least may) come to greater fruition at a later time. But he went further than both those theologians in that he treated infant regeneration as an *actual* regeneration and opened the door to a genuine apostasy from baptismal grace so that the child lost *status salutis*. Baptized infants have been incorporated into Christ and have the root of faith "secretly lodged in the heart, and seen to God, though not sensible to the man himself"; however, baptismal regeneration is not always followed by future grace. Baptismal grace is sufficient to enable perseverance, but only efficient to that end in the case of the elect. Regarding infant salvation, Bedford concluded: "I shall not make any doubt but the infant is regenerate in baptism, justified and freed from the guilt and dominion of sin: consequently [he is] saved if he die in his infancy."[6]

### The New England Way and the
### Origins of American Revivalism

Puritans in the New World eventually moved toward considerably different views. The "New England Way," as it came to be known, downgraded the place of the sacraments in defining the people of God. Church membership came to be based more and more on subjective experience, divorced from objective covenant boundary markers (such as baptism). According to Philip Benedict,

> the Church of Boston first amplified experimental predestinarianism's confidence that the elect could discern the signs of grace

---

5. See Holifield, 150, for these data on Cotton and Hooker.

6. Hans Boersma, *Richard Baxter's Understanding of Infant Baptism: Studies in Reformed Theology and History, New Series, No. 7* (Princeton: Princeton Theological Seminary, 2002), 11–12, 74–75.

within themselves into a requirement that candidates for church membership testify about the working of grace in their soul. By 1636, the restriction of church membership to such "visible saints" was the norm among New England churches.

The results of tightening up church membership were predictable.

> By restricting church membership to those who could offer testi-mony of saving faith [in the demanded manner], the New England way ensured that only a fraction of residents would be full church members . . . In time the percentage of church members tended to decline, as many of the younger generation raised within the church found it difficult to discern internal evidence of saving faith. [7]

New England's harsh rigorism, designed to protect the church, actually threatened to destroy the churches altogether. It was a suicidal para-digm. The church created a new ritual (or sacrament?)—the require-ment of a personal and public profession of faith and testimony—in order to obtain communing membership. It was no longer adequate simply to profess to trust Christ as Lord and love His people; one had to profess to be *converted*. This was especially intimidating to children, who were essentially treated as non-members (not just non-communicants) under the new paradigm.

People still went to church on a regular basis, but the masses were treated as outsiders, especially in the rhetoric of the sermons. (Of course, civil law generally required attendance at preaching services even for those who were not communing members!) In some cases, people still went to church because they were actually believers, though the church would not acknowledge them as such because they hadn't had the prescribed experience, or were too timid to narrate their testi-mony to the elders. By today's more relaxed standards, these people would probably have been admitted to the table in most evangelical churches. However, their faith—or at least their assurance—was man-gled by hyper-introspectionism.

---

7. Philip Benedict, *Christ's Churches Purely Reformed: A Social History of Cal-vinism* (New Haven and London: Yale University Press, 2002), 390–91.

The New Englanders eventually came to believe that God dealt with every sinner in basically the same way, whether coming out of a Christian home or rank paganism. God worked through the understanding to reach the will and emotions. In addition, the sinner passed through an intense period of Spiritual preparatory work as God began convicting him of sin. This was sometimes referred to as the "spirit of bondage" of a "law work" in which the sinner was made to feel and grieve his inability and depravity. Finally, after much agonizing of soul, the sinner could be released into the freedom and joy of the gospel, though this assurance of grace, so hard to come by, could be lost easily through negligence or willful sin. Everything was attuned to experience and feelings, and as those fluctuated, so did assurance. The Puritans continued to pay lip service to older Reformational models that based assurance on the objective promises of Scripture directed to faith and sealed in the sacraments, yet now the emphasis was almost entirely on an inward, deeply-felt change of heart. Even outward conformity to the law of God was no guarantee one was in a state of grace apart from fulfilling the experiential paradigm. Obviously, this view excluded the covenant succession model set forth by Calvin and the other early Reformers. It was no longer possible to grow up Christian.

Thus, the New England Way was no friend of covenant children. Someone who gave David's testimony in Psalm 22:9–10 would have been turned away in New England's churches. There was an internal contradiction in the New England Way in that families generally raised their children in an environment of piety and truth, but that kind of nurture made it improbable that the children would grow up to have the very kind of dramatic experience that the New England Way required of them in order to become full church members! In other words, their patterns of familial devotion and their demands for experiential conversion were working against one another. This left Puritanism open and vulnerable to the worst influences of creeping revivalism, beginning with the First Great Awakening.

The net effect of this shift was a deep divide in the church between those who were "holy enough" to come to the table, many of whom were no doubt prideful hypocrites, and the rest of the congregation, comprised of "half-Christians," many of whom probably should have been regarded as true believers. As the former group shrunk and the latter group expanded, the church moved more and more to the margins of the culture. The new "visible saints" idea of the church clashed with the original Puritan vision of a holy commonwealth.

The older model did not deny the importance of a Spirit-wrought work of grace in the soul. There must be heart-felt conviction, transformed affections, love for God and neighbor, and so on. Nevertheless the new view abstracted experience from the environment of the covenant rather than contextualizing it within the framework of the covenant. In the old pattern, children were regarded as church members (albeit non-communing members) even apart from experience. Admission to the table was granted on the basis of a profession of faith and a life that conformed outwardly to Christian standards. These were things men could judge and evaluate. In the new practice, elders had to be able to read hearts—or at least pretend to do so. In the new way, children weren't really members of the church at all, even after baptism; at most, baptism placed them in a sort of holding tank until they were old enough and mature enough to have the kind of experience church elders and pastors were looking for. Often, the descriptions of what composed a "true work of grace in the soul" became maddeningly complicated and nuanced. Preachers aimed at tearful conviction of sin followed by the ecstatic joy of salvation. Many entered the first phase without ever reaching the latter because assurance was hard to come by in the highly introspective, emotionally-charged environment of revivalism. The result of revivalist methods was a shoehorning of everyone's experience into the same model and a loss of appreciation for the variety of ways the Spirit can work to draw a sinner to the Savior. Even worse, the covenant nurture paradigm of the Psalter and the gospels was almost completely lost.

While the New England Way underwent various changes in the seventeenth and eighteenth centuries, it made a lasting mark on the shape of American church life. Indeed, the First and Second Great Awakenings in the eighteenth and early nineteenth centuries can be regarded as the full flowering of the New England Way. In the twentieth century, revivalism evolved from the "saw dust trail" and camp meetings to Billy Graham crusades and evangelistic campus ministries.

There were various adjustments made, but the intense focus on individual experience only open to older people was a common thread.

Eventually, the techniques and practices of revivalism came to be institutionalized in American churches in various ways. For example, in the revivalistic program of Charles Finney (1792–1875), theology was replaced almost entirely by psychology as the "New Measures" (such as the anxious bench) were geared to elicit an emotional response under pressure. This was just the outworking of Finney's Arminianism, in which revival was simply the "right use of constituted means," making it the work of man as much as the work of God. In the revivalism of Dwight Moody and Ira Sankey, sentimentalist music was combined with highly emotional, anti-intellectual preaching to put listeners in the right frame of mind for having a "conversion experience." Everything was aimed at getting the sinner to make the all-important "decision" for Christ.

Pietism, fundamentalism, and contemporary evangelicalism all have roots deep in the soil of American revivalism. For the most part, the revivalist/conversionist paradigm completely replaced the covenant nurture/paedofaith paradigm in American churches. While the evangelistic zeal of these movements is to be appreciated, they have often been lacking in theological substance. They represented dramatic, deliberate, and decisive steps away from historic Reformed theology and church practice. Their decided tendency is to define Christianity in almost exclusively emotional and individualistic terms. The inconsistencies of the seventeenth century Puritans were resolved, in the main, by moving in a Baptist direction. Revivalism was totally hostile to a doctrine of paedofaith.[8]

## Jonathan Edwards

Jonathan Edwards deserves mention in this survey not only because of his historic stature and contemporary popularity, but also because his view appears to straddle the fence between the older Calvinian view of

---

8. For a comprehensive examination of revivalism's tendencies and features, see Peter Leithart, "Revivalism and American Protestantism," in *Christianity and Civilization, Volume 4: The Reconstruction of the Church* (Tyler, TX: Geneva Ministries, 1985), 46–84. Leithart admits the effects of the revivals were not all bad. Revivalism has not totally lacked redeeming qualities. But, overall, it still represents a significant distortion of biblical Christianity.

paedofaith and the emerging revivalistic view of covenant children which was gaining momentum in the eighteenth century.

Edwards believed God could work saving grace in the heart of an elect infant. He was open to the possibility that some infants dying in infancy receive salvation. Edwards wrote, "The infant that has a disposition in his heart to believe in Christ if he had a capacity and opportunity is looked upon and accepted as if he actually believed in Christ and so is entitled to eternal life through Christ."[9] Infants can be regenerated and united to Christ as "potential" believers. This "disposition" to believe possibly could be construed as closely akin to Calvin's "seed" of faith, though in greatly weakened form. Even more so than Calvin, however, Edwards distinguishes the infant's disposition to faith from the adult's actualized faith. The gap has widened. For Edwards, infants might possess an openness to faith, but it is latent at best. There is no true capacity for faith until the child matures, even though God (mysteriously) reckons him as though he actually did believe, and thus gives him a title to eternal life. Here Edwards is moving toward a position of infant salvation that is an exception to *sola fide*, although he is somewhat ambiguous. After all, how is a *disposition* to faith different from faith itself?

Unfortunately, Edwards did not apply his theology of infant faith with much consistency. He was typically skeptical of Spiritual experiences on the part of children who lived beyond infancy. He was willing to acknowledge the genuineness of his wife's juvenile experience of grace around age four or five, and he did the same with a young girl

---

9. Quoted in Gerald McDermott, *Jonathan Edwards Confronts the Gods: Christian Theology, Enlightenment Religion, and Non-Christian Faiths* (New York: Oxford University Press, 2000), 137. See also Anri Morimoto, *Jonathan Edwards and the Catholic Vision of Salvation* (University Park, PA: Penn State University Press, 1995), 30ff, 62f. Morimoto demonstrates the complexity of Edwards' bundle of convictions. On the one hand, "few are converted in infancy" because grace must be "sensible and visible." On the other hand, Christ has compassion on infants and removes the "disadvantages" of infancy. Morimoto also argues that Edwards' view of "dispositional faith" in infants is akin to the faith of an adult who is asleep. It is genuine faith, but is not being actively exercised. Thus, infants dying in infancy might be saved on account of an inactive disposition. This is a substantially messier and more tenuous account of infant faith than Calvin offered. Edwards used his latent/active faith distinction to argue against early child communion, since the Supper supposedly requires active faith.

named Phoebe Bartlett during a local revival, even though such youthful piety was not regarded as the norm; indeed, these were highly unusual cases. The little Bartlett girl may be the exception that proves the rule that the revivals were generally unkind to covenant children. For Edwards, youthful piety was rare. A child growing up in the faith from his earliest days was regarded as abnormal. Even if it was considered a possibility, youthful piety would not be recognizable until later in life and thus children were not given the benefit of the doubt. Most covenant children, in Edwards' paradigm, would not experience grace and salvation (and therefore become "communing members" of the church) until much later in life. Because grace must be "sensible" or outwardly evident, children have little chance of proving themselves to their Spiritual examiners. Of course, it was this experience-centered type of piety that aided and abetted the rise of the Halfway Covenant in New England and accelerated the disintegration of Puritanism.[10] Edwards op-

---

10. For historical background to the Halfway Covenant, consult Edmund Morgan, *Visible Saints: The History of a Puritan Idea* (Ithaca and London: Cornell University Press, 1963). On Edwards' relationship to New England's Halfway Covenant theology, see Iain Murray, *Jonathan Edwards: A New Biography* (Edinburgh: Banner of Truth, 1987). The debate over the Halfway Covenant traced back a century before Edwards and revolved largely around admission to the Lord's Table on the basis of "experimental Christianity" and whether or not the children of non-communing adult members of the Church were eligible for baptism. The issues are complex, of course, but it is clear that most theologians in Puritan New England lost any sense of the objectivity of the covenant and the efficacy of the trans-generational covenant promises. A distorted view of covenant children eventually came to dominate American Reformed theology and produced numerous irregularities.

For example, nineteenth-century Presbyterian stalwart and Princeton professor Samuel Miller married a girl who had been raised in a Christian home but had never become a "professing Christian" nor had been admitted to the Lord's Table because she had not had the requisite internal experience. Revivalism excluded many from the means of grace because of its demand for a certain kind of experience. Eventually Miller's wife claimed tentatively to have had the needed experience, hoping she had "given herself to Christ." But even then she was filled with doubt and hesitation as she approached communion. It was not for another three years before she came into a state of certainty, claiming to finally rest "on a firm gospel foundation." Revivalism gave the impression that the "normal" Christian life would be a life of constant doubt that could only be cured through intensely emotional experiences of grace. Revivalism often made grace hard to come by, especially for those reared in Christian homes, for whom

posed the Halfway Covenant, even as his type of theological and pastoral rigorism made it an almost inevitable development. The Halfway Covenant's apparent laxity was just an equal and opposite reaction to the more high-strung Puritans.

In the theology of Edwards, Puritan experientialism reaches its zenith, for good and bad. His emphasis on Christian affections, meditation, the sweetness and beauty of God, and a warm devotional life are refreshing countermeasures to the Reformed tendency toward arid rationalism in theology. His zeal for prayer, church renewal, and the social application of Christianity are also commendable. Edwards sought to be a balanced theologian and pastor—much more so than many of his theological contemporaries and heirs. He sought to correct what he perceived to be the flaws of Christians in his time and place. but he lacked a fully biblical grasp of the covenant promises and the efficacy of the sacraments. With no objective toehold for faith to latch onto, Ed-

---

a dramatic change in life would be less likely. See David Calhoun, *Princeton Seminary: Volume 1* (Edinburgh: Banner of Truth, 1994), 67f.

As revivalism first emerged, it was routine for children to get baptized as infants, grow up in Christian homes, regularly attend church and participate in family worship—without ever openly rebelling—and still never come to the Lord's Table or becoming "full" members of the church because they had not passed through all the stages required by revivalism's theology of conversion. For example, Archibald Alexander grew up in a Christian home, attending a church pastored by a Princeton-trained man. In his late teen years, a Baptist friend asked if he had experienced the new birth. "Not that I know of," Alexander replied, for he had never heard this experience mentioned among the Presbyterians. Then one Sunday night, while reading John Flavel to the Baptist family he was tutoring, he had an overwhelming Spiritual experience. He came to regard this as his conversion. (The Baptists were no doubt thrilled to have converted a Presbyterian!) See Iain Murray, *Revival and Revivalism: The Making and Marring of American Evangelicalism 1750–1858* (Edinburgh: Banner of Truth Trust, 1994), 93–95. Alexander actually went on to doubt the propriety of paedobaptism for several years afterward before solidifying his place in the Presbyterian fold. Nevertheless, he would go on to argue that, while sanctification from the womb or baptismal font is possible, it is far from the norm. Instead, because cases of baptismal regeneration and pious children are so rare, "The education of children should proceed on the principle that they are in an unregenerate state, until evidences of piety clearly appear." This is the basic principle of revivalism. See Alexander's *Thoughts on Religious Experience* (Edinburgh: Banner of Truth Trust, 1989 reprint), chapter two.

wards' style of ministry inevitably drove people inward for assurance. The question "Am I in a state of grace?" was answered not by looking to Christ and seeking Him in the community or the external means where He promised to make Himself available; instead, it became a matter of taking stock of internal desires and motions of the soul toward God. Not even an evaluation of outward obedience was all that helpful. While self-examination certainly has a place in the Christian life, Edwardsean piety, like most of later Puritanism, made too much of it.

Edwards' over-emphasis on experience as a barometer of one's Spiritual condition, severed from an objective understanding of the covenant and sacraments, made assurance too delicate and placed a question mark over the heads of covenant children. Unfortunately, the worst features of Edwards' theological program were expanded upon and developed in American revivalism. His Calvinism was forgotten, and his theology of the affections degenerated into sentimentalism and emotionalism. Edwards' theology tended to downplay the biblical themes of paedofaith and covenant succession. The hyper-emphasis on a conversion experience led to a decline in attention given to the nurture of covenant children in their infancy and youth.[11]

### Nineteenth Century American Reformed Theology
*North vs. South*

Many Presbyterian pastors had the good instincts to oppose revivalism when it first emerged, but it eventually won out and took over the American church. In the eighteenth century, in the wake of the First Great Awakening, Presbyterians found themselves divided between the anti-revival "Old Side," emphasizing the ordinary means of grace, the value of a "settled" ministry, the importance of the church's doctrinal standards and discipline, and a high view of the corporate church body, over against the pro-revival "New Side," emphasizing personal piety, individual experience, itinerant evangelistic ministers, a more democratic view of church authority, and a voluntaristic ecclesiology. Presby-

---

11. Of course that makes it rather ironic that the Edwards family is one of the greatest *illustrations* of covenant succession in American history. One generation after another in the Edwards family tree served God faithfully in the church and world. See Murray, *Jonathan Edwards,* for details.

terians formally split over the issue in 1741, then reunited in 1758, with the New Side revivalists clearly in the driver's seat. Revivalism has been the distinctive flavor of American evangelicalism ever since (though with some significant exceptions). Obviously, this mix of revivalistic convictions and practices made little room for a discussion of paedofaith.

Nineteenth-century American Reformed theologians were so committed to rationalistic epistemologies (e.g., Scottish common-sense realism) that they could not consider seriously the question of infant faith. While the question did come up from time to time, it was largely eclipsed by questions surrounding conversion. Indeed, conversion had become the major feature and central topic in Reformed theology and practice.

This is not to say these theologians were uniformly hostile to covenant children. On the balance, the nineteenth-century Southern Presbyterians were much more negative than their Princeton counterparts in the North. The Southern church was more influenced by the revivalists' view of children, whereas Princeton took a more balanced view of the revivals, encouraging deep Christian experience, but seeking to ground it in biblical truth. The Princeton theologians saw revivalism as a potentially healthy corrective insofar as many Presbyterians had a tendency to divorce theology from experience. They acknowledged the real problems that had cropped up from the indiscriminate practice of paedobaptism and the lack of familial nurture. They sought (however imperfectly) to sort out the good from the bad in the revivalistic movement.

The Southern church imbibed more deeply and less discerningly the implications of revivalism for covenant children and sacramental theology. James Henly Thornwell, a leader in nineteenth-century Southern Presbyterianism, said baptized children were to be regarded as any other enemies of Christ until conversion was evidenced by signs of the new birth. For him, baptism was a non-effective sign which, at most, put a thin dotted line between our children and the world. By contrast, Princeton systematic theologian Charles Hodge insisted that baptized children were to be regarded as church members, under God's favor and care from infancy onward. He said they should be regarded as members in the same way that their parents are, on the basis of presumptive election, presumptive regeneration, and presumptive membership in the invisible church.

The issue came to blows over the proposed 1857 revision of the Presbyterian Book of Discipline. Consistent with his principles, Thornwell said that baptized children were not to be subject to the discipline of the church. Only those who had made a profession and came to the Lord's Table were really under the oversight of the church. Non-communicants could not be excommunicated. They were never branches on the tree, so they could not be cut off. Thornwell considered baptized children to be a separate class of church members from professors, and said their church membership was only accidental. They did not belong to the essence of the church.[12]

In counterpoint to Thornwell, Hodge and others said baptized children were to be included in the visible church on the same basis as adults. They were Christian children and were to be raised as such. They were covenant members, subject to the covenant's blessings as well as its sanctions. Hodge's arguments were not stated as well as they could have been, but he certainly had Reformed history on his side.

This debate pointed to a deeper theological divide. The issues included conflicting theologies of conversion, sacramental efficacy, ecclesiology, and so forth. According to Thornwell, the great task of the church was the conversion of her children. Baptized children are in the church, but only in an external and formal way; as far as their heart and life are concerned, they are of the world. For Thornwell, making a profession of faith was virtually equivalent to claiming to be converted. Thus, he demanded that children "pass the test" of conversion "which changes their status." Until then, they are spiritually dead. Again, Thornwell's position was clearly a departure from historic Presbyterianism in favor of revivalism. Thornwell was single-handedly suggesting a complete redefinition of the church in Reformed theology. He was completely evacuating the sacrament of infant baptism of its efficacy as an effectual means of salvation. Hodge and his allies were able to forestall Thornwell's revisionary project, and the debate was never resolved because the church divided into Northern and Southern factions in

---

12. That the Southern Presbyterians were headed in an Anabaptist direction at this point in history is also seen in the fact that they became the first Calvinists in history to reject the validity of Roman Catholic baptism.

1861. The separated churches did, however, go on to produce their own books of discipline. The Northern church eventually ended up rejecting Thornwell's most radical revisionary proposals, while the Southern church basically adopted his position on covenant children.

In many parts of America, especially in the deep South, Presbyterians continue to have strong revivalistic tendencies. Indeed, these tendencies are often as powerful and pervasive among Presbyterians as among the Baptists. Presbyterians will baptize their children, but then, like the Baptists, wait until their children have the needed law/gospel experience, or pray a conversion prayer, or manifest evidence of the new birth, in order to regard them as "real" church members. When Presbyterian pastors do church membership interviews with new families, even if the families have been lifetime Presbyterians, they are almost just as likely to inquire as to when and how the prospective members were converted, automatically ruling out the possibility that they grew up Christian.

*The Mercersburg "Reformed and Catholic" Movement*
A refreshing exception to nineteenth-century American revivalism was found in the "Mercersburg Movement," led by John Williamson Nevin and Philip Schaff. While Nevin had a revivalistic background (he was "converted" at age fourteen under the preaching of Asahel Nettleton), he turned against it as he imbibed more and more classical Continental Reformed theology. He had been Hodge's star student at Princeton, but afterwards moved well beyond Hodge in seeking to recover and revitalize the older Reformed theology of Church and sacrament. Schaff was a German immigrant with a brilliant mind and an incredible breadth of knowledge. What made Nevin and Schaff so distinctive was their "Reformed Catholic" approach. They viewed the Reformation not as a radical break with Medieval Christendom, but as its true child. The Reformation was the next phase in God's unfolding plan to bring the historical Church to maturity, though American Protestantism's radical individualism, sectarianism, and anti-traditionalism were gross distortions of the true meaning of the Reformation.

Nevin and Schaff were marginalized and attacked, but they did not allow that to intimidate them into silence. They wrote voluminously to propagate their views. They argued that the Church is the Mother of all

Christians, and that the Church, therefore, makes individual Christians rather than the reverse. We do not give life to the Church; She gives life to us. God extends grace through the outward means of Word and sacrament. American preoccupation with individual salvation and anti-sacramental piety were regarded as compromising the catholicity and churchliness of the biblical gospel.

Related to our topic in this book, Nevin and Schaff both argued for a high view of sacramental efficacy and a covenant nurture model for Christian parents. Rather than making a point of conversion the basis of Christian identity, they argued that Christian identity should be inculcated in our children over time through prayer, catechesis, and sharing in the common life of the church. Nevin argued:

> Infants born in the Church are regarded and treated as members of it from the beginning, and this privilege is felt to be something more than an empty shadow. The idea of infant conversion is held in practical honor; and it is counted not only possible, but altogether natural that children growing up in the bosom of the Church under the faithful application of the means of grace should be quickened unto spiritual life in a comparatively quiet way, and spring up numerously "as willows by water courses" to adorn the Christian profession, without being able at all to trace the process by which the glorious change has been effected.[13]

For all practical purposes, this is a doctrine of paedofaith. By grace, children share in the organic faith-life of the church. Whereas the revivalists addressed their ministries exclusively to adults, Nevin viewed Christian children as fit recipients of salvation through the church's means of grace. They were to be gradually enculturated into a life of Spiritual conversion, beginning with baptism. Thus, the church grows not just from the outside, through external additions, but also from the inside, as children are conceived in her womb. The church is the supernatural elevation and transformation of human life in its wholeness and fullness in Christ Jesus. As a new creation, the church must (like the old creation that she takes up into herself to transform

---

13. Quoted in Glenn Hewitt, "Nevin on Regeneration," in *Reformed Confessionalism in Nineteenth Century America* (Lanham, MD: Scarecrow Press, 1995), edited by Sam Hamstra, Jr. and Arie J. Griffeon, 159.

creation that she takes up into herself to transform and renovate) include children, including infants.

Nevin, however, was very critical of those who, like Horace Bushnell, tended to tie salvation into nature rather than grace. Nevin accused Bushnell of turning baptism into nothing more than a symbol of the natural, organic connection between parents and children. It involved no transaction of divine grace. Nevin was ecclesiocentric and holistic, over against Bushnell's familiocentrism and (alleged, at least) dualism.

Nevin also differed from Old School Presbyterians in how he critiqued revivalism. Whereas Hodge argued against revivalism primarily on the basis of his Calvinistic soteriology and doctrine of the decrees, Nevin held to a softer and more ecclesially-shaped version of Calvinism. He based his case against the revivalists on his theology of the Church and sacraments, not predestination. He argued that revivalism was an attack on the gospel precisely because it distorted the catholic substance of the gospel. Revivalism's false theology of the church showed itself in a misunderstanding of both the incarnation and the sacraments. Thus, he labeled it "Antichrist" in his book of that title.

While Nevin and Schaff were largely voices crying in the wilderness, they stood as a witness against the radical Americanizing of the church through the revivalist movement. They were an often unwanted reminder that the American church had largely gone its own way, seriously departing from the historic Reformed tradition and the catholic faith. However, the fact that the movement so quickly fizzled out showed that America was not really ready for a broad scale Reformed catholic church movement. Things would have to get even worse before they could get better.

### Current Discussion

After long neglect of the Bible's paedofaith theme, the pendulum is beginning to swing back. In recent decades, many Reformed theologians have been willing to reassess the possibilities and probabilities of infant faith. However, there is still no consensus among scholars working in the Reformed tradition. Paedofaith remains a much-vexed and controversial issue.

Many theologians today who see infant faith as a legitimate possibility do not view faith as an infused habit as the older theologians did. Instead, they see faith as a relational disposition to trust. Thus the question is not, "Can infants receive a certain *habitus*, or capacity, for faith?" but "Are infants capable of having interpersonal relationships?" Faith is still regarded as a divinely-given gift of grace, but in light of a more relational view, infant faith seems more "natural" (that is, more on a continuum with other relationships) and less of an oddity. In this context, the link between parental nurture and the sprouting of paedofaith into full-grown, fruitful faith is strengthened.

Moreover, in this relational view, a "seed" of faith is not "latent" or "passive" faith, compared to "actualized" or "realized" faith that comes later in life. Rather, it is "baby faith" compared to the "adult faith" that comes with greater maturity. The infant's seed of faith is real faith, not just potential faith. It is a faith, however, that needs to grow over time, as the child matures.

The discussion over paedofaith is sure to continue, but more and more thoughtful theologians across denominational lines are finding themselves open to paedofaith as normative within the life of the church. Without tying the doctrine too closely to child studies, psychology, epistemology, communication theory, and work in other various academic disciplines, Christians should be open to seeing what they can glean from these other fields that will help us as we wrestle through the question together.

More and more Christian parents are thinking through the implications of raising their children in a secular world and are finding the presupposition of paedofaith a biblically and practically attractive position to take. It is not at all surprising that the collapse of Christendom in the West would prompt a reassessment of the question of paedofaith and covenant nurture in general, given that Christian parents must now begin to rethink what it means to bring up godly offspring in a hostile host culture. We can no longer take it for granted that the wider culture will help us as we train our children; indeed, the forces of the culture are arrayed against the Christian parent. The Christian parent needs every available advantage and encouragement; a well-formulated, biblically-grounded, and practically-articulated doctrine of paedofaith could be of great service to covenant families. Whereas the revivalist model wastes the first several years of the child's life waiting for a spectacular conversion experience, the paedofaith/covenant nurture model takes full advantage of this impressionable period by impressing a Christian identity and way of life on the child from the beginning. Because the child has faith, this is simply reinforcing the work of God's Spirit and makes the parents partners with the Spirit in the work of covenantal nurture.

Paedofaith also meshes well with recent research into the emotional and cognitive development of infants. Scientists are finding that infants actually learn best (and perhaps only) in the context of human relationships. They need an emotional bond to the one who teaches. Even from their earliest days, infants already manifest rich and varied emotional lives. They are able to experience empathy, frustration, joy, sadness, and jealousy. They can read facial expressions and detect the differences between actual human communication and artificial forms of stimulation, like television and recordings. These findings are as tentative as any other scientific research, but it is certainly worth noting that they reinforce precisely what many Christians have believed and known all along: infants are imago Dei, fully relational creatures, able to interact with others even before they have learned how to talk. Moreover, these investigations remind us of another biblical truth, namely, the importance of communicating love and building relational trust from the child's birth. But unless we are going to regard Christian Spirituality as an additional layer of life, placed over a natural, non-religious core, in some secondary way, then we must also be open to discussing the Spirituality of infants. A relationship with God is not "added" to a natural human life at some later point; it is intrinsic to human life at all times. If the Christian gospel is more than a tacked on "extra" to natural human life-if it rehabilitates and transforms the fallen creation as a whole, bringing it to eschatological fullness-then there is no reason to think infants or small children are somehow outside the scope a redemptive relationship with God. In our final two chapters, we will look at infant Spirituality in relation to church and family life. We have much to gain by developing a more thorough understanding of how God works in our covenant children.

# seven

# connecting the dots:
## paedofaith and life
### in the covenant community

What are the implications of this doctrine of paedofaith? If the arguments made thus far are persuasive, several important items follow. Paedofaith inevitably has a bearing upon Christian praxis. In this chapter we will examine paedofaith in relation to paedobaptism, paedocommunion, and the tendency toward rationalism in the Reformed tradition. We will find paedofaith affirms paedobaptism, opens the door to paedocommunion, and challenges all rationalistic, ideological distortions of the Christian life. In the following chapter, then, we will look at a matter of supreme significance, namely, paedofaith in relation to the vocation of Christian parenting. We will see that understanding paedofaith is critical to tackling the challenges of raising faithful covenant children.

## Paedofaith and Paedobaptism

First, if our doctrine of paedofaith has been derived from sound exegesis of the biblical texts, the practice of paedobaptism is more securely established. I have argued elsewhere that the logic of paedobaptism depends, at least to some extent, on maintaining a high view of baptismal efficacy.[1] Here we can further buttress that thesis by pointing out that the rationale for paedobaptism also depends upon paedofaith, at least to some extent. (Obviously these are just two ways of saying the same thing since faith is necessary to receive the grace of baptism. If paedobaptism logically depends on baptismal efficacy, and baptismal efficacy hinges on faith, then everything comes down to the possibility and presence of paedofaith.)

How does paedofaith relate to paedobaptism? It simply makes no sense to say that God has authorized us to baptize unbelievers. Everything in Scripture seems to connect faith to baptism (cf. Mk. 16:16). Insofar as paedobaptism is regarded as a faith*less* baptism more often than not, the practice slips away and the Baptist case is strengthened. If paedobaptism is biblically warranted, paedofaith must be a reality.[2]

In this way, we can say the efficacy of infant baptism is as universal as the presence of infant faith. Baptism is an "effectual means of salvation" (WSC 91) to believers. Baptism becomes an efficacious means of judgment in the case of those who do not receive baptism in faith. *However, if we have reason to regard a particular baptized child as a believer, we have no reason to doubt the efficacy of his baptism. If we have reasons to doubt he is a believer, we have no business baptizing him.*

Thus, we can join with the declaration of Calvin's children's catechism. Calvin includes these questions and answers pertaining to baptism:

Q.   My child, are you a Christian in fact as well as in name?
A.   Yes, my father.

---

1. See "Paedobaptism and Baptismal Efficacy" in *The Federal Vision*, edited by Steve Wilkins and Duane Garner (Monroe, LA: Athanasius Press, 2004), 71ff.

2. Thus far, we can agree with Jewett: "To baptize infants apart from faith threatens the theological foundations of evangelicalism" (162). Of course, Jewett is quite wrong when he immediately follows up that statement by arguing that baptism is man's work, rather than God's enacted promise. Nevertheless, all of Jewett's arguments on pages 160–65 should be weighed carefully by paedobaptists who wish to maintain their practice while simultaneously denying paedofaith.

Q.  How is this known to you?
A.  Because I am baptized in the name of the Father and of the Son and of the Holy Spirit.

Q.  How did you come into this communion of the Church?
A.  Through baptism.

Q.  What is this baptism?
A.  It is the washing of regeneration and cleansing from sin.

Obviously, Calvin is presupposing the presence of faith or else he would deny that the one baptized received these blessings offered in the sacrament. Calvin's children's catechism trains the child to think of himself as a believer from infancy.

Martin Bucer, Calvin's close friend and theological twin, included this language in his baptismal prayer:

> Almighty God, heavenly Father, we give You eternal praise and thanks, that You have granted and bestowed upon this child Your fellowship, that You have born him again to Yourself through holy baptism, that he has been incorporated into Your beloved son, our only Savior, and is now Your child and heir.

Again, this baptismal teaching only works if paedofaith is presupposed. Bucer's liturgy implies paedofaith.

The French Reformed baptismal liturgy makes the point with great eloquence. At a baptism, the pastor would speak these words to the child:

> Little child, for you Jesus Christ has come, He has fought, He has suffered. For you He entered into the shadows of Gethsemane and the terror of Calvary; for you He uttered the cry "it is finished." For you He rose from the dead and ascended into heaven, and there for you He intercedes. For you, even though you do not yet know it, little child, but in this way the Word of the Gospel is made true, "We love Him because He first loved us."

These are not declarations one would make over an unbeliever. Indeed, apart from a strong doctrine of paedofaith, such affirmations can only be calculated to produce hypocrisy and presumption. Admittedly, the child does not know the gospel in its propositional form (e.g., 1 Cor. 15:1–11), but he is nonetheless embraced in a living, loving relationship with God as His heavenly Father.

Craig's Catechism, an important document in the Scottish Reformation, taught the following:

Q. What if our children die without baptism?
A. Then they are saved by the promise.

Q. Why are they baptized, when they are young and do not understand?
A. Because they are of the seed of the faithful.

Q. What comfort do we have in their Baptism?
A. This, that we rest persuaded that they are inheritors of the Kingdom of Heaven.

Q. What should that work in us?
A. Diligence in teaching them the way of salvation.

Q. What admonition are they given through this Baptism?
A. That they are to be thankful when they come to age.

Q. What then is Baptism for our children?
A. An entry into the Church of God, and to the Holy Supper.

This is an excellent summary. Our children belong to God even before baptism, but baptism is their actual entrance into the kingdom and church. Children are baptized on the basis of the covenant promise. In baptism, the promise that they are heirs of God's kingdom comes to realization. When they come of age they are not called upon to convert, but to express gratitude at God's gracious provisions, given even before they were able to profess faith in an external way. Finally, baptism is the basis of parental diligence. We are not to be presumptuous but to direct our children continually in the way of salvation, training them to walk life's path in steps of faith and repentance.

These are only a few samples. We see this sort of thing consistently in the classic Reformed tradition. Catechetical materials tie the child's kingdom membership and salvation to the covenant promises and baptism. Strong baptismal assertions are made over the newly baptized child—assertions that only make sense in a context of faith. Apart from faith, these sorts of declarations would be lies and fairy tales because apart from faith the sacraments do not bring salvation. Indeed, to receive baptism apart from faith only leads to harsher judgment. If our children are unbelievers, it would presumably be much safer to "wait and see" as the Baptists do than to subject them to the conditions and sanctions of the covenant.

Infant baptism, paedofaith, and baptismal efficacy are a package deal. They reinforce and strengthen one another. Or, as Cornelius Van Til would say, these doctrines mutually imply one another. Infants belonging to believing parents are fit recipients of baptism precisely because they have faith; and because they have faith, their baptisms are efficacious.[3] They can use baptism rightly because God has already established a relationship of trust with them.

Paedofaith helps to build an impregnable wall around the doctrine and practice of paedobaptism. The major objections to paedobaptism are related: a) the infant does not possess faith, the prerequisite for baptism (the Anabaptist objection); and b) infant baptism imposes a religious identity on an unwilling subject (Karl Barth's objection).

By now we have seen that Scripture counters both these arguments. If children are believers, they ought to be baptized. They meet the required condition. Scripture warrants this claim in several passages. Moreover, if the children of believers have been given "baby faith" by the Spirit, infant baptism does *not* impose on them a foreign religious identity at all. Rather, it goes *with the grain* of their pre-given orientation toward God. Paedofaith means our children are not opposed to God or even neutral toward Him; they are inclined to Him in a relationship of

---

3. As noted earlier, this view of baptismal efficacy obviously opens a rather large can of worms, especially for those not initiated into the current Reformed discussion. Unfortunately, at this juncture we cannot get all the worms back in the can. For more background, see my essay "Baptismal Efficacy and the Reformed Tradition: Past, Present, and Future" available at http://www.hornes.org /theologia/content/rich_lusk/baptismal_efficacy_the_reformed_tradition_past_ present_future.htm.

trust and love, however immature they may be. Because God has given our children this nascent faith, teaching them God's truth is not a matter of brainwashing or indoctrination; rather, it is giving them just the kind of nourishment they need to grow and flourish in the faith they already possess. We should expect receptivity as we teach them with patience and love because God's Spirit is already at work in them.

We should learn to couch our understanding of covenant children in light of the reality of paedofaith. Sometimes we speak of the church as composed of "believers and their children"—as though these were two separate classes of people—adult Christians (who have faith) and their children (who are baptized, but not regarded as believers until later in life). It may be appropriate to distinguish *professing* believers from their children (who cannot yet verbally profess their faith) as the Westminster Confession does (WCF 25.2), but we should not regard our covenant children as unbelievers unless and until they prove themselves to be so. The church is simply the community of the faithful and our children are part of the church. God's promise and Christ's declaration ensure that fact. Of course, deadwood may show up in the community from time to time, and it has to be pruned away. Not every church member turns out faithful, and so church discipline is a necessity, but three-year-old apostates would seem rather unusual in a healthy Christian church. Again, there is no reason to put our young covenant children in the category of "covenant-breaker." We must view them through the lens of the covenant promise.

We should also revise the common terminology that contrasts "believer's baptism" with infant baptism. This concedes the high ground to the Baptists since it is easy enough in Scripture to show a link between faith and baptism (Mk. 16:16). We should avoid giving the impression that Baptists believe in baptizing believers while paedobaptists do not. Instead, we should grant to our Baptist brethren that *only believers* should be baptized, and then we should issue the challenge: prove (in light of all the evidence adduced above, from both Old Testament and New Testament) that our covenant children do *not* have faith! Baptists may not be willing to grant our reading of these texts, but neither should we grant their premise that they baptize believers while we do not.

This is the ground on which our discussion with Baptists should take place: Do children of the covenant have faith? Has God made them promises? The debate is *not* over whether or not it is acceptable to baptize unbelievers, provided they come from believing parents. There is only one kind of baptism in the church; adult believers and infant believers receive the same baptism.

The paedobaptism/paedofaith connection also bears upon how we raise our children. Paedobaptism-based parenting is a topic we will take up in the last chapter. Here we will briefly note that Calvin (*Institutes* 4.16.32) saw infant baptism as a powerful motivating force behind faithful and attentive parental care.

> It is precisely this which Satan is attempting in assailing infant baptism with such an army: that, once this testimony of God's grace is taken away from us, the promise which, through it, is put before our eyes may eventually vanish little by little. From this would grow up not only an impious ungratefulness toward God's mercy but a certain negligence about instructing our children in piety. For when we consider that immediately from birth God takes and acknowledges them as His children, we feel a strong stimulus to instruct them in an earnest fear of God and observance of the law.

We baptize our children because we believe God's promises about them. Believing those promises includes believing they have faith, and if our children are *God's* children, and already trust in Him, Christian parents have no excuse to be ungrateful or negligent, and every incentive to instruct them in the fear of God and fidelity to His law.

Paedofaith and paedobaptism are based on God's covenant promises. In the covenant, God says, "These children are mine!" He claims them for Himself. He makes them members of Christ's body in baptism. As such, we must teach them that they are Christians from their first days. We must raise them as Christians, educate them as Christians, disciple them as Christians, discipline them as Christians—in short, we must treat them as Christians in every way. The covenantal nexus between paedofaith and paedobaptism provides us with a theological lens through which we can see clearly what God would have us do with our (or really, *His*) children.

Christian parenting that takes its shape from these doctrines continually asks questions such as, "What does my child's baptism mean to him and for me? What was his condition before baptism? What happened at his baptism? What is my task in light of his baptism?" These sorts of questions will be answered by believing what God says about the child. God is his God; he is a member of the kingdom; he is holy; he is united to Christ. This is the touchstone of the parenting task and the blueprint according to which parents should build.

### Paedofaith and Paedocommunion

Second, the practice of paedocommunion is made more plausible by this doctrine of infant faith. While paedocommunion seems very odd to most modern Western Christians, it has a long and venerable history. The Eastern Church has always practiced paedocommunion. While the origins of paedocommunion in the West are hotly debated, we can trace paedocommunion virtually as far back as we can trace paedobaptism. Moreover, everyone agrees that paedocommunion was the generally accepted practice in the West up until the twelfth century, when the dogma of transubstantiation caused it to fall into disfavor.[4] In recent decades, there has been a revival of support for paedocommunion by leading theologians in every major paedobaptist tradition. This movement continues to build momentum.[5]

If paedofaith is biblically defensible, the arguments for paedocommunion become almost overwhelming (if they aren't already!). Of course, this almost goes without saying. Aside from highly questionable

---

4. For an overview of the history of paedocommunion, see Tommy Lee's essay, "The History of Paedocommunion: From the Early Church to 1500," available at http://www.reformed.org/sacramentology/tl_paedo.html.

5. Here is a sampling of paedocommunion's wide appeal in the contemporary church—Presbyterians: Peter Leithart, Robert Rayburn, Jack Collins, G. I. Williamson; Methodists: William Willimon, Laurence Hull Stookey; Episcopals/Anglicans: Ray Sutton, N. T. Wright, David Holeton; Lutherans: Scott Marcincic.

exegesis of 1 Corinthians 11:28,[6] the most frequent Reformed objection to paedocommunion is that our covenant children lack the faith necessary to participate meaningfully in the Supper. Because they lack faith, the Supper is at best just an ordinary meal for them, and at worst actually places them under a curse.

However, if our arguments in this work hold up under scrutiny, this objection has been defeated. If our children do in fact have faith, there can be no bar to their joining with us at the Lord's Table. To add further requirements beyond faith (or even to insist that faith must attain to a certain maturity level) before granting access to the covenant meal is a practical denial of *sola fide*. It turns the table (implicitly, at least) into something that is earned rather than freely given. James White explains:

> One can hardly bar baptized children from the table without questioning their baptism itself. If they have been united to Christ and incorporated into the Church through baptism, one can hardly say that sharing in Christ's death and resurrection do not count until they understand it. What God does in baptism for infants or for adults is not done halfway. It is a lifelong gift that places us completely within the priestly body.
>
> Neither sacrament is a reward for faith but a means to its development. The presence of children at the Lord's Table reminds adult Christians of how much growth lies ahead of us all. Could it be that this is children's special form of priestly ministry as the whole community gathers around the Lord's Table?[7]

If our children have faith, and the purpose of the sacrament is to strengthen and increase faith (cf. WCF 14.1), then paedocommunion is virtually a logical corollary of paedofaith. To withhold the Supper from them is to starve the very faith we are called to feed and nourish. We need them at the table to remind us that the bread and wine are free gifts.

Paedofaith forces us to rethink what church membership means for our children. If we have biblical reasons for regarding our children as

---

6. For pro-paedocommunion exegesis of this text, see Tim Gallant, *Feed My Lambs* (Grand Prairie, Alberta: Pactum Reformanda Publishing, 2002), and Jeffrey Meyers, *The Lord's Service*, 367–96.

7. White, 67.

"little believers" (Mt. 18:6), then we have compelling reasons to include them in the church's covenant renewal feast. To exclude them is a matter of sheer prejudice. The church must not practice age discrimination (or ageism, as it has been called). Paedocommunion is fully consistent with Reformed principles of ecclesiology. It is just an embodiment of the covenant membership of Christian children.

To say that faith must be expressed a certain way, or must be "active" as opposed to merely "passive," or "mature" rather than "immature," simply will not work as an objection to paedocommunion. Our covenant children have the ability to receive Christ's blessing at the table every bit as much as the infants in Matthew nineteen could receive blessing from His touch. Christ wants to receive our children at His table every bit as much as He wants to receive them in the waters of baptism. He says, "Let the little children come to me." Who are we to refuse them? To withhold the Supper from them is to deny them something that belongs to them as faithful members of the covenant. They are being put wrongly under the censure of excommunication. The only pre-Eucharist requirement placed upon a baptized child is the ability to eat and drink. Anything else hinders them from coming to Jesus, contrary to Matthew 19:14. If we reject paedocommunion, we are acting like the disciples who tried to keep the children away from Jesus.

### Paedofaith versus Christian Rationalism

Third, infant faith strikes at the heart of all of rationalistic versions of Christianity. Biblical faith is not reducible to an ideology. Certainly, there are doctrines and concepts to master, and we do not want to downplay the importance of maintaining systematic and propositional truth for the health of the church.

However, we also need to make sure the pendulum does not swing the other way, as it often has. All too easily, the post-Enlightenment Reformed church has fallen prey to a kind of theological legalism, in which salvation comes (at least implicitly) through doctrine. This reverses the traditional Augustinian epistemology which underlies the great theological contributions of men like Anselm, John Calvin, and Cornelius Van Til. Augustine said, "I believe in order to understand."

Applied to the question at hand, this is the point: as the faith of our children matures over time, they will come to a fuller understanding of the place and importance of Christian doctrine. *Yet lacking understanding does not prevent them from exercising faith; indeed, as they exercise their faith in an ever-growing way, their understanding begins to develop toward fullness.* To require our children to have understanding first is to put the cart before the horse. It is to lapse back into the Greek notion of the primacy of the intellect.[8]

This also means that we need to make room at the Lord's Table for the mentally deficient and the senile. There are some people who simply will never come to a mature understanding because their reasoning abilities are impaired. When such persons are part of a believing family and a Christian church, it is simply preposterous to keep them from the table because they can't understand or explain the meaning of the bread and wine. They probably *can* understand, in all kinds of non-cognitive ways, what it means to be included (or excluded) from a family meal.

---

8. We need to think through the full humanity of our children. Human personhood is not defined by intellectual or verbal capacities, as critical as those faculties are. James White is insightful. "In recent years, the developmental sciences have taught us much about how children perceive things. We know that they recognize relationships long before they deal with abstract concepts. Thus, one is forced to ponder whether Christianity is basically a system of doctrines, as adults tend to believe, or whether there is something more fundamental to it, such as relationships of love within a community of people. Any child could tell us, 'Church is people.'

"Psychologists now assure us that children perceive much long before they develop conceptual ways of knowing. A child as early as six months old can know what it is to be included or excluded, especially when food is being distributed. Long before they arrive at levels of analytical reasoning, children have a profound understanding of relationships of love. The five-year-old granddaughter of a United Methodist bishop, being asked why she went to the Lord's Table, replied, "To say hi to Jesus." That comes closer to the truth than many adults could formulate using much more sophisticated language about Christ's presence. To exclude baptized children from the Lord's Table on the grounds that they do not fully understand it would, if we followed such an argument out, exclude us all. One does not understand a mystery, one experiences it. And children reared in the community of faith can experience it as well as anyone, perhaps better than some of their adult associates." See *Sacraments*, 66. While we should be careful to base theology on Scripture, not science, it is interesting that contemporary children's studies are, at least in some cases, coming to conclusions that mesh quite well with a biblical view of childhood.

God is not cut off from forming and maintaining a relationship with them. Thus, they should have access to the sacraments even if (or maybe especially because) the Word cannot do all that much for them. The intellect is not God's only gateway into a person's heart. They need to be at the table with us to experience the presence of their heavenly Father (cf. Lk. 24:30–31).

I am also shocked and dismayed that some Presbyterian and Reformed pastors actually contemplate excommunicating older Christians who drift off into senility either because of age or Alzheimer's disease.[9] This reveals just how rationalistic we've become.

The problem with all of these sorts of cases (infants, the mentally challenged, the elderly) is compounded by the fact that these are precisely the categories of people we're called to give special honor to in the church. We've already seen how Jesus singled out children with special favor, setting a model for us. In 1 Corinthians 12:22–25, Paul reminds us that the weakest members of the body are not an embarrassment to the community; instead, they are essential to the health of the community. If these members are lacking in honor, it is up to the rest of the body to compensate by heaping an extra measure of honor upon them. It is hard to do this when we are excluding them from the feast.[10] If anything, they ought to have seats of honor at the Lord's Table. If we refuse to allow them to eat with us, we are reversing the value

---

9. I once had a conversation with a Reformed pastor who strongly objected to my views of infant faith because (in his mind) it required a complete recasting of the traditional definition of faith. In order to try to make my point another way, I asked him about an aging Christian who had walked faithfully all his life, but in the twilight of his years became unable to articulate any theological truth or mentally digest preaching. "Would you continue to serve such a person the Supper, or would you excommunicate him?" This pastor thought long and hard before finally answering, "I don't know." Consistency, of course, requires treating both ends of the spectrum of human life in the same manner. If infants are excluded from the Supper because they lack articulated, intellectually formulated trust, then the aged must be excluded on the same grounds.

10. I may be jeopardizing my own credibility by citing him, but Gary North's essay "The Excommunication of Ronald Reagan" is a witty and provocative look at this issue as it relates to Christians who eventually contract Alzheimer's disease. The article is available at http://www.degenhart.us/Articles/Reagan.htm. North's point is that Alzheimer's and infancy are made into disciplinable offenses by current Presbyterian practice.

scale the Lord has given to us (cf. Jas. 2:3).[11] Children at the table stand as witnesses against legalism in all its forms, whether moral/ethical or rationalistic/doctrinal. Their very helplessness reminds us that the table is not just for the strong and mature but also for the weak and helpless. It is a table of free grace.

---

11. We often overlook how much infants and mentally handicapped people can *contribute* to the life of the church, even in their passivity. If the saying of Jesus is true, "It is more blessed to give than to receive" (Acts 20:35), then their presence as needy members of the body provides a wonderful field of opportunity for the rest of us to experience the blessing of *giving* love, friendship, and care to those who cannot provide for themselves. The whole body is strengthened as it cares for its weakest members. For an example of this, see Peter Leithart, *Priesthood of the Plebs* (Eugene, OR: Wipf and Stock, 2003), 154n27.

# eight

## *paedofaith and the*
## *task of christian parenting:*
### *going with the grain of the covenant*

Obviously, paedofaith has important implications for parental nurture. This is a topic I have already broached in an earlier article on baptism,[1] and full treatment would require something like a more lengthy book. Here in this closing chapter we will only sketch out some of the more prominent features of Christian parenting as our calling to raise children up in the fear and admonition of the Lord is related to the biblical doctrine of paedofaith.

### The Nature of the Covenant Child

To begin, we should note that parents must have a grasp of the nature of the child they are called to disciple. The children of Christians should grow up Christian. This Christian identity is not age or ability dependent. Baptized children should be nurtured in the faith from the beginning of life. We cannot help children grow into a covenantal identity

---

1. "Paedobaptism and Baptismal Efficacy," 109ff.

unless we know their identity as covenant members and impress it upon them. In this case, *nature*—the nature of the child—requires *nurture* as a way of life. Nature and nurture come together in the covenant. The task of Spiritually nurturing the child goes with the grain of his covenantal identity and nature.

How can we know our children are believers? Not from inspecting their hearts. Often, not even from examining the fruit in their lives or their profession (though as they grow older, these external tests become more important indicators, as they are for adults). Rather, parents *know* their children are believers because they are actively *trusting* the covenant promises themselves. They derive the faith of the children from their own faith in the trans-generational promises of the covenant. They parent by faith, from faith, and to faith.

If parents take the covenant promises to heart, they will not become presumptuous. Faith, after all, bears fruit. Faith obeys God's commands and trembles at His threats. Faith without works is no faith at all. For example, those who believe God's promises about prayer become diligent in prayer. Likewise, those who believe God's promises about children are diligent in raising their children in the ways of God. They will not "let go and let God." They will not take anything for granted.

Neither will they fret and worry over the Spiritual condition of their young children. Faith brings assurance. Thus, they will not manipulate their children into praying a prayer or making a decision. Instead they will rest in the covenant, knowing that God loves their children even more than they do. Those who have such faith will pray, teach, and discipline with confidence and consistency. They will have a peace and stability in their parental work. Without faith, however much parents may do these things, they are simply works of the flesh and cannot be effective in the long run.

Christian parents must learn how to raise their children up with a covenantal identity, alternately comforting and challenging them. Our children must be brought up under the aegis of the cross and the Spirit. We will hold their hand as their youthful, tender faith is tried, and we will push them to ever greater levels of maturity as they grow. Constant nurture in the context of family life will bring our children along the way God calls them. We will help them to become more and more who they already are in principle in Christ Jesus. James White ties several of these important threads together:

> Frequently, the baptized children of Christian parents grow up never knowing themselves to be anything but Christian. They may not like theoretical predestination, but many live by a practical one. Their being brought to baptism through the concern of Christian parents is an act of fulfillment of God's will for them. They know the Church as insiders. Through baptism God has made them insiders, not onlookers. Becoming what God has made them, Christians, goes on largely in the family. This is why every threat to the family today also endangers the traditional means of shaping new Christians. Such threats undermine the best locale for catechesis Christians have ever known, the family.
>
> Christianity, after all, is more than a theology; it is a way of life, a network of relationships of love. To include children in the Christian family and yet exclude them from membership in the body of Christ [e.g., the Lord's Supper], seems inconsistent. If children cannot be part of God's community being saved, it is dubious whether adults belong there either . . . Baptism goes much deeper than intellectual cognition alone. It is not contingent upon our maturity and cognitive abilities. Rather, it changes our whole life within a context of loving community relationships, expressed both in family and in the Church.[2]

God uses the created structure of the family to pass the faith on from one generation to the next. The function of the family in covenant succession is paramount. God promises to work through parents in a special and effective way as they trust in His promises about their children.

However, no family is self-sufficient, and no family can effectively disciple its own children apart from participation in the life of the broader church family. *It takes a church to raise a covenant child*, we might say. Our ultimate identity as Christians is lodged in the faith-family of the church, not the biological family (Mk. 3:34). This is why the church (not the family) normally performs baptisms. In terms of day-to-day responsibilities for the nurture and care of God's covenant children, however, the family is the central social institution. The church disciples

---

2. White, 47.

the family in a general way, but parents are responsible for their own children in a way no one else can be.

### Raising God's Children

Our children belong to God. Through the covenant promises, ratified and sealed in the sacrament of initiation, God makes our children His own. In other words, all Christian parents are really foster parents: *we are raising Somebody else's children.* Our children are God's special possession (Ezek. 16:20; Mal. 2:15; Mt. 18:10–14), and we will be held accountable for raising them according to His standards. As Bucer said, if we do not expend the greatest pains and effort in bringing our children up to obey Christ, then we are guilty of robbing God of His children. In effect, we hand them over to Satan.

Parenting is a form of stewardship. But God does not put Christian parents in the impossible position of having to kindle faith from nothing in the hearts of their children. He gives Christian children a spark of faith that parents will either fan into a flame through diligent nurture, or douse through carelessness and laxity. The heart of covenant nurture, of course, is giving our children the gospel as the story they live (and die) by.

This is precisely how the Bible's most comprehensive instruction on parenting works. In Deuteronomy 6:1–9, 20–25, we find that the first responsibility parents have (after loving God themselves) is diligently and constantly teaching their children about God's work of redemption on their behalf.[3] This is what it means to teach them Torah: it is to press into them the story of what God has done and how we should respond (Deut. 6:20–25). It is simply a given that this story of redemption belongs to our children as much as to us. All parental instruction begins and ends with the imparting of this gospel narrative. For the Israelites, this meant teaching the exodus story; for us, it means teaching the new covenant exodus in Christ. But the pattern is unchanged.

On the basis of this redemptive narrative, parents are to impress upon their children holistic instruction from God's Word: the forehead

---

3. See also Deuteronomy 4:9 on these two priorities of a) parents obeying God's Word from the heart; and b) teaching their children to have the same loyalty.

(thought/worldview), hand (work/play), doorpost (family life), and city gate (public life) are all to be marked with God's Word. In other words, our children are to live in an atmosphere permeated and saturated with the stories and principles of God's revelation in Scripture (6:8–9). Parents are not to do this intermittently, but simply as a way of life, using every possible occasion as an opportunity for carrying on this work of education (6:7). They are not to be slack or sloppy in it, but diligent, in both formal and informal modes of instruction (6:7). To put it briefly, parents must sanctify the time and space their children indwell by surrounding them with the Word of God, spoken, embodied, enforced, and exemplified. Parents must remember: *everything matters to God.* Their teaching should be constant and comprehensive.[4]

Parents are not simply to give their children a form of morality, but are to root carefully and explicitly the Christian way of life in the story of redemption (6:20–25).[5] This is their ultimate task. This is the key to

---

4. There are many practical ways to do this. Parents should recognize that life is full of opportunities for "by the way" instruction. We should talk to our children constantly, helping them to learn what it means to interpret the world in Christian terms and categories. This also means reading to our children early and often. Live by the maxims "You are what you read" and "He who reads, leads." We should read only the best quality literature to our children, but should do so in massive quantities. We should make liberal use of Proverbs since it is the Bible's book of fatherly counsel for sons (and daughters). We should emphasize biblical stories and the singing of psalms. Regular times of family worship (especially singing) and catechesis are also important. Sadly, I have known families who intentionally delayed starting family worship until their children were "old enough" to fully understand and actively participate. This is why understanding Scripture's paedofaith theme is so important.

While the matter of formal education is often complex, parents should strive to give their children the most Christian form of education available to them. On the importance of Christian education, see the provocative and thoughtful works of Douglas Wilson, including *Recovering the Lost Tools of Learning: An Approach to Distinctively Christian Education* (Wheaton, IL: Crossway, 1991); *The Paideia of God and Other Essays on Education* (Moscow, ID: Canon Press, 1999); *Excused Absence: Should Christian Kids Leave Public Schools?* (Mission Viejo, CA: Crux Press, 2001); and *The Case for Classical Christian Education* (Wheaton, IL: Crossway, 2003).

5. Robert Louis Dabney rightly emphasizes the importance of parental instruction in a covenantal context. "Here is the parent's responsibility, and here also is the encouragement. Our God is a faithful and a righteous God. He has not laid this heavy and fearful burden upon our shoulders without the promised help to bear it. His covenant still stands, to be a God to His people and their seed.

covenant succession (cf. Ps. 78). Children who are given rules without the underlying story are the first to forget the rules the moment they leave home. The moralism their parents passed on to them has no solid foundation; it is a house of cards, and can be (at best) propped up by self-righteousness. It cannot produce a life of faithfulness, integrity, joy, and service.

If we fail to constantly teach our children the gospel, we will still be teaching them—but we will be teaching them that the stock market, baseball, and Disney are all more important than Jesus. Parents teach inescapably, and if they aren't proclaiming Christ to their children, they're proclaiming something else. Silence about Christ is just another form of dogma, every bit as insidious as a heresy, cult, or rank paganism.[6] If we fail to teach our children the infinite value of Christ, we end up teaching them He is of no value at all.

Because our children are included in the life of faith from the beginning, parents do not have to *wait* to begin giving their children Christian nurture. Indeed, the very early years of childhood are often the most important and impressionable period of life. Certainly advertisers recognize this, even if Christian parents sometimes do not! Par-

---

Faithful effort and holy example shall be rewarded . . . By the very reason which makes parental neglect so blighting to the souls of children, parental teaching will prove an efficient help.

"Seeing the parental relation is what the Scripture describes it, and seeing Satan has perverted it since the fall for the diffusion and multiplication of depravity and eternal death, the education of children for God is the most important business done on earth. It is the one business for which the earth exists. To it, all politics, all war, all literature, all money-making, ought to be subordinated; and every parent especially ought to feel, every hour of the day, that, next to making his own calling and election sure, this is the end for which he is kept alive by God—this is his task on earth." From *Discussions of Robert L. Dabney, Volume 1: Theological and Evangelical* (Edinburgh: Banner of Truth Trust, 1967 reprint of 1891 edition), 691. Perhaps overseeing a congregation as a pastor or elder is of slightly greater importance than parenting children. In both cases, eternal issues are at stake. But otherwise, Dabney is exactly right in stressing the importance of parental obligations. In no other area of life will we so directly influence whether or not another person goes to heaven or hell. Dabney's argument echoes the priorities of Deuteronomy 6: love God yourself, and train your children to be faithful to Him as well.

6. I think this point comes from John Piper, but my memory will not allow me to place it with certainty.

ents must begin cultivating covenant fidelity the day they get home from the hospital with their newborn baby. Jesuit missionary Francis Xavier said, "Give me the children until they are seven, and anyone may have them after."[7] In other words, by seven years old, the concrete is basically set and children have been riveted into a trajectory that will carry them the rest of their lives. Horace Bushnell actually viewed the age by which the die was cast as three! Charles Hodge said more is accomplished before the child learns to talk to permanently affect his character for good or ill than all that is done in the following years.

To be sure, these claims are a bit hyperbolic. While there certainly is not an absolute rule here, there is much proverbial wisdom (Prov. 22:6). It is easier to bend a twig than a full-grown tree, after all. Thus, we need to initiate the process of Spiritually shaping our children from the very beginning. Parents who trust God's promise that their children are believers will be in a good position to do so. Many Christian parents unfortunately expect nothing good from their young children, and so they are not diligent in the early years; their pessimistic outlook then becomes a self-fulfilling prophecy. By the time they should be setting their children free from detailed rules, they start multiplying rules like crazy to try to reign in wayward teenagers. The parents have sown wild oats in their children, and all they can do now is pray for crop failure.[8]

Paedofaith is also an important dynamic in the discipline of our

---

7. Quoted in Donald Van Dyken, *Rediscovering Catechism: The Art of Equipping Covenant Children* (Phillipsburg, NJ: Presbyterian and Reformed, 2001), 92. I highly recommend this book as a guide to the critical practice of catechesis.

8. This is not to say parents can never make up for lost ground if they have made a mess of things, but it is very hard work. Parents must begin by confessing sin (to God and their children) and repenting. They should then try as best they can to deal with their children where they are. They should also pray fervently, asking God to graciously fulfill the covenant promises in the lives of their children despite parental shortcomings.

All parents are sinners, of course. No parent deserves to have children who turn out well and no parent should take even a speck of credit if his kids do grow up to walk faithfully. Parents who nurture by faith know this and will thank God for whatever they accomplish. But the Bible does acknowledge varying degrees of covenant fidelity among parents (e.g., Eli's failure in 1 Samuel) and does establish a general (however inscrutable) connection between the quality of parenting and the way the children live as adults (e.g., Prov. 29:15).

children. If we refuse to discipline our children, we are really refusing to disciple them. We are preparing them for apostasy more than perseverance (Prov. 13:24). Giving children what they want is incredibly dangerous. God entrusts parents with the rod so they can teach their children the consequences of sin in a vivid way (Prov. 19:18). God mysteriously connects pain inflicted on the body's backside with the shaping of the heart. Children must learn that the way of the transgressor is hard. They must learn the way of obedience is the path to blessing. They must come to see that they will reap what they sow. They must be discipled to make practicing love of God and neighbor habits of the heart.

If we do not use the rod (or equivalent), we will misshape our children's faith.[9] God will become an indulgent Santa Claus-in-the-sky or a great cosmic vending machine to them. They will be decidedly self-centered rather than sacrificial in their life-orientation. As we faithfully and lovingly discipline our children, we remind them that they are branches on the vine, but they must be pruned to bear fruit (Jn. 15:1ff). This discipline may be painful, but it serves a good purpose, as it promotes their holiness (Heb. 12:5ff).[10] Parents who must administer seemingly endless rounds of discipline should not grow faint or begin to doubt the covenant promises; instead, they should remind themselves that while their children are believers, they are immature, and discipline is one of the best means through which growth toward Christ-likeness is accelerated. They should not give up the fight or grow weary in doing what is right; instead, they should continue to be patient, consistent, and lovingly firm. Every use of the rod is an opportunity to further im-

---

9. For more on the proper use of the rod, Tedd Tripp's book *Shepherding a Child's Heart* (Amityville, NY: Calvary Press, 1995) has many helpful thoughts. Tripp emphasizes the importance of dealing with the root of sin in our children, not just external behavior. Parents should administer correction in a context of humility, charity, and consistency. Tripp's book is from a Baptist perspective, but thankfully, he expects God's Spirit to be at work through parental means of teaching and discipline.

10. Puritan Cotton Mather put it well: "Better whipped than damned." That is essentially the point in Hebrews 12 and in Proverbs. Without discipline, our children will inevitably drift from the path of life and go to hell. The same is true of adult Christians, of course. If we forsake the nurture and discipline of the Church (our mother), we will end up abandoning the faith altogether.

press upon children the gospel narrative as we move them from confession of sin to God's forgiveness in Christ, and back to their response of faith and repentance.

Because our children are believers, we should handle parental discipline in much the same way we would handle church discipline. We should confront our children about their sin, and help get to the heart (literally) of the issue. We should administer correction with gentleness (cf. Gal. 6:1), and afterwards seek to restore fellowship. We should also lead them in seeking God's forgiveness and help in prayer. At every point we should deal with them as fellow Christians put under our care. Painful episodes of discipline should be short interruptions in an otherwise joyful family environment.

### The Calling of Christian Parents: Conversion or Discipleship?

So what is the Christian parenting project? Christian parents are called to create a Spiritual culture in the home that will incubate their children in the life of faith, hope, and love from their earliest days. Christian parents are more like pastors shepherding their flock than like missionaries trying to convert heathen. Indeed, paedofaith stands against all forms of conversionism which put certain models or types of experience at the center of the Christian life. Conversionism assumes that our children do not have a relationship with God until they have had their own conversion experience and have decided for themselves to embrace Christianity. In a conversionist paradigm, a child must convert through an act of the will once he has reached an age of understanding. It is impossible to grow up Christian from infancy. There must be some sort of decisive crisis conversion experience.

Certainly, experience, like doctrine, is important and has its place, but it cannot be totalized. Indeed, we cannot always trust our own experiences any more than we can always trust our reason; we need something outside our experience to provide an interpretive framework against which our experience can be measured and evaluated and categorized.

Faith in mature form includes both sound doctrine and conscious experiences of God's grace, but it is deeper than both. The Davidic paradigm in the Psalter shows that growing up in the covenant does not *require* a dramatic conversion experience; indeed, such an experience might be a sign something has gone terribly wrong somewhere along the way.[11] Likewise, in the new covenant, the experience of Timothy shows that covenant nurture-unto-perseverance is still the norm for children of believers in the messianic era (2 Tim. 3:14–15).

This is *not* to say that a doctrine of paedofaith denies the reality of a subjective experience of God's grace. Certainly, we expect our children to have a wide variety of experiences of God's grace as they grow up under His covenant care and nurture at home and in the Church. The covenant has a subjective side, and for the blessings of the covenant to be realized, they must be received by a living, vibrant faith. As that faith grows and matures, the child will experience faith at work overcoming trials, resisting temptation, seeking the Lord's guidance through prayer, and so forth. At times the child may be overwhelmed with the reality of God's grace, and at other times the child may experience a period of coolness. There may be crisis points through which God's grace is experienced in unique and fresh ways. But the child should not be trained to seek after or expect a dramatic *conversion* experience from unbelief into faith as the absolutely necessary mark of true religion.[12] This expe-

---

11. The Psalter is so helpful at precisely this point because it holds together the objective and subjective sides of the covenant. On the one hand, David views his infancy, and indeed the rest of his life, through the lens of the objective covenant promises. The psalms can serve to train our emotions in the way God desires. On the other hand, the Psalter records numerous "renewal" experiences in David's life. Those who emphasize the objectivity of the covenant (that is, what is true even apart from our conscious experience) should be careful not to overly downplay or minimize experiences (even dramatic and mystical experiences) of God's grace. The covenant, of course, provides the context and backdrop against which these experiences should be interpreted.

12. The analogy of marriage is obviously helpful here. A couple may have all kinds of wonderful experiences over the course of a lifetime together. But none of those experiences usurp the place of the wedding day, the objective event that brought them together as husband and wife. In fact, that objective transition in states is the basis for all subsequent experiences. The objectivity of the covenant does not cancel out Christian experience, but gives it solid footing. Those covenant children raised in believing homes who are taught to think of a certain experience in later years as their conversion (e.g., when they got involved in a college ministry) are like a couple that confuses their second honeymoon with their wedding day.

rientialism has been the bane of much of American evangelicalism, going back to some of the more extreme Puritans, and especially the revivalists of the Second Great Awakening. This sort of thing has been in
the bloodstream of American Christianity for a long time.

When Christian parents think in terms of conversionism, two
things happen. On the one hand, the pressure for the child to conform
to preset notions of what he should experience can be tremendous. The
child, consciously or subconsciously, feels the need to match his experience to the norms and models imposed upon him from the outside. In
fact, studies have shown that Christian children reared in various traditions more often than not have precisely the kinds of experiences that
their tradition expects them to have!

On the other hand, there is a temptation for parents to think that
once their child has had the sought-after experience and been admitted
to the Lord's Table, their work is basically done. The child has had the
needed "salvation experience" and now has a "fire insurance policy" in
his back pocket, come what may. Without revivalistic conversion, the
child has nothing; after the conversion experience, he has everything.
But this focus on a one-time experience of conversion truncates the fullness of the Christian life. The chief end of life is reduced from glorifying
God and serving neighbor to simply "getting saved." Conversionism
often makes too much out of conversion and too little out of a subsequent life of holy obedience.

Parents who treat their children as believers from the outset are
able to counter these problems, if they are faithful in their task. On the
one hand, they are able to make it clear in very tangible ways from the
child's earliest days that everything about the Christian life starts with
God's gift, not our achievement. For example, the Lord's Supper is not a
reward for making a profession or having an experience. Rather, it is a
sign and instrument of God's grace, offered to the covenant child from
his youth. God washed the child in baptism to prepare him for the table.
He's a member of the covenant family.

On the other hand, such parents are (or at least should be) less likely
to be presumptuous because they understand that while the whole process of Christian growth may start in infancy, it is never completed in this
life. The parent's job is not to get the child to make a one-time profession

or pray a "sinner's prayer"; instead, the parent's calling is to produce a mature, full-orbed disciple over an eighteen- to twenty-year period. Parents do not need to wait for a revival or a "conversion experience" to begin teaching and training their children in holiness and Christian habits. Parents should get to work Spiritually nurturing right away. The more quickly covenant character formation takes place, the fewer sinful routines there are to unlearn later on in life. The means of grace help the parent do this, but the vigilant parent will remind himself and his children never to take those means for granted (1 Cor. 10:1ff). The child will be taught to renew the baptismal covenant regularly through a sustained, lifelong course of repentance and participation in corporate worship, including the Eucharist.

Of course, I'm not saying paedofaith (or paedobaptism or paedocommunion) automatically creates good parenting or that the conversionist position precludes good parenting. It is never that simple. But these are trends. The appalling rate at which we lose our covenant children to the world, even from good, solid Reformed churches, should at least make us open to re-assessing what we have said about infant faith, parental nurture, baptism, and admission to the Lord's Table. Paedofaith and paedocommunion are not "cure-alls" for what ails us, but they would seem to be part of the prescribed medicine. Revivalism taught us far too high a view of feelings and momentary experiences and far too low a view of the sacraments, the nurture of parents in day-to-day life, and the pursuit of holiness in ordinary routines. It is time to correct both these excesses and deficiencies.

### Covenant-Based Parenting

This doctrine of paedofaith should be seen as an aspect of a broader covenant theology. We were chosen to the covenant in order that we might direct our children in the same faith we have been given (Gen. 18:19). Our children are born into the lap of the Church. God is their Father and the Church is their Mother. The promises God has made to and about our children (Gen. 17:7) do *not* mean that our children are good prospects for evangelism, or that they are *potentially* Christians, or that we can expect that *someday* our children will embrace the covenant for themselves through a conversion experience. This way of thinking turns the covenant promises inside out. The point of God's transgenerational mercies is that our children *already* belong to Him and know Him from the earliest possible age. This is the heart and essence of promise-based parenting.

Without a doctrine of paedofaith, there is a huge hole in our doctrine of the covenant—a hole out of which the smallest members of the covenant fall until they climb back in by running through whatever gauntlet we set for them (memorizing a catechism, going through a communicant's class, passing an elder examination, having a "narratable" conversion experience, etc.).

When God declares that He has saved His people, He always includes their children in that redemptive work (Gen. 6:18; Ex. 12:26–27; Deut. 6:20–25; 7:7–11; Isa. 59:21; Acts 2:38–39; etc.). It is simply unthinkable that God would say to us, "I love you, but I'm not interested in a relationship with your children." No, even in human relationships, to love a person ordinarily includes caring for his whole family. Thus, God's promises are not to individuals alone, but for familial units.

These promises are the bedrock of faithful Christian parenting. Parents need a sturdy foundation on which to build, and the covenant provides it. A promise is a promise, especially when made by God. Parents can count on God to keep His Word. As Calvin pointed out again and again, God's covenant promises include the salvation of our children. Indeed the promises were made for this very reason: that we might know that God loves our children and desires their salvation.

By standing upon the rock of these covenant promises, parents are able to establish a sound pattern of covenantal nurture. They are able to train their child up inside the sphere of Christian faith so that he will live his whole life there. The project set before Christian parents is not a one-time conversion experience but to get their child in a set pattern of lifelong discipleship. Note that the proverb does *not* say, "Train up a child in the way that he should go and when he is old, he will *enter* into it" but "when he is old, he will not *depart* from it" (22:6). In other words, the proverbial principle here is not that a child who grows up under covenantal nurture will eventually convert from unbelief to faith; rather, the point is that he will not abandon the faith in later years because of the good foundation laid in his youth. Covenant nurture is unto perseverance, which presupposes that the covenant child *begins* in a place of grace and faith.

Similarly, in Ephesians 6:4, Paul does not instruct Christian fathers to bring their children up *into* the training and admonition of the Lord, as though they were outsiders. Rather, they are brought up *in* the Lord's way, since they are already members of the covenant people, the communion of the saints (as Paul's immediately preceding exhortation to the children implies in 6:1–3).

The covenant is a solid base for Christian parenting to rest upon. Some invent an "age of accountability" doctrine because they cannot bear the thought that their unbelieving children are outside the pale of God's salvation.[13] The "age of accountability" theory is used to soften

---

13. Arguments for an age of accountability rest on very thin Scriptural support. Appeal is made to passages like Deuteronomy 1:39, which speaks of those who are too young to know (or determine) good and evil for themselves, and Numbers 14:29, where God says those under age twenty will enter the promised land, unlike their parents who will perish in the wilderness because of their sin. To be sure, the Bible does recognize varying levels of maturity, and with greater maturity comes greater responsibility. But these passages do not establish an age of accountability. (If they did, they would prove too much since it is rather obvious that kids make their own decisions before age twenty. It would be morally disastrous to tell a teenager he will not be held responsible for any actions performed before twenty years!) Knowing good and evil in Scripture has to do with making mature judgments. It has to do with rule and wisdom and office, not accountability per se. If this kind of knowledge is necessary to accountability, then Adam and Eve should not have been held accountable for their sin in Genesis three. The Tree of the Knowledge of Good and Evil represented entrance into mature, eschatological rule and judicial office. Adam and Eve claimed that office prematurely (Gen. 3:22). But obviously Adam and Eve were expected to make responsible decisions before God granted them access to the Tree! We see "knowledge of good and evil" language connected with royal office in several places. Solomon, as an adult, prays that he might have knowledge of good and evil so he may rule wisely (1 Kings 3:9). In Isaiah 7:15–16, the royal child does not know good and evil until he is old enough to enter into his office. In Genesis 24:50, Rebekah denies Laban judicial power to determine a case with this sort of language. And so on. See Cornelius Van der Waal, *The Covenantal Gospel* (Neerlandia, Alberta: Inheritance Publications, 1990), 49ff for a full discussion.

In addition, the age of accountability doctrine suffers from (theo)logical contradiction. If all children are "saved" in their youth because they are morally innocent and unaccountable, then they "lose" their "salvation" when they commit their first actual sin. Or, to look at it from another angle, all pre-mature children (those who have not yet reached the age of accountability) are elect and

what Scripture teaches about original sin and the just wrath of God against our children. But there is no neutrality in God's universe. If our children are not believers, from infancy onward, they belong to Satan and stand under God's curse. If the promises of the covenant do not place them under the redeeming, propitiating blood of Christ from infancy, we must regard them as damned. Those who reject paedofaith must be prepared to live with the pastoral and parental consequences of rearing children who do not know God.

But my hunch is that this cannot be done consistently. After all, virtually all Christian parents pray with their children, teaching them to call on God as "Father" from an early age. We sing "Jesus Loves Me" with them, which only inculcates presumption and hypocrisy unless we actually regard them as believers. We take them to church with us because we have (at the very least) an intuitive sense that God accepts them into His presence and that they should be present when God's people gather. They are part of the new covenant family, set apart from the world. We motivate our children to obey not just with threats of punishment, but with appeals to God's grace. We catechize them in ways that implicitly teach them to treat the gospel as their own possession (e.g., Heidelberg Catechism 1; WSC 44, 100).

Participation in the sacramental life of the covenant community (including both baptism and the Eucharist) is fully consistent with these other means of nurture, though here our inconsistency often starts to show itself.[14] A doctrine of paedofaith encourages us to raise our children so that they never know a day when they did not trust in the Lord and rely on His goodness, especially as that goodness is felt and tasted at the font and table. They grow up in the culture and social life of God's people.

---

would go to heaven if they died. But then they lose this elect status as soon as they reach the age of accountability and become lawbreakers. Clearly, this is not the Bible's teaching! The Bible certainly has a doctrine of apostasy, but this is not how it functions.

14. For a more extended discussion of parental nurture and paedocommunion from a more aesthetic perspective, see my essay "For the Children's Sake" at http://paedocommunion.com/articles/lusk_for_the_childrens_sake.php.

Thus, paedofaith is a doctrine with solid biblical grounding, adequate historical support in the Reformed tradition, and immense practical value. While there are mysteries and ambiguities involved, this is true of every Christian doctrine. Let us thank God for the firm covenant He has given us—a covenant that includes our children in the life of faith and the sacramental gifts of the kingdom. Let us seek to nurture our children, bringing their paedofaith to full maturity in Christ.

### Paedofaith: A Summary

What does the doctrine of paedofaith mean? We cannot summarize everything here, but we will try to lay out the most salient points of the Bible's teaching, setting paedofaith in the context of the Bible's wider covenant theology. This is not intended as a precise confessional statement, but rather one last way of tying everything together for the convenience of the reader.

1.  God graciously includes the children of at least one believing parent in the covenant of grace. The covenant promises are not made merely to individuals but to families. They are trans-generational and corporate. This is because the covenantal program of salvation is rooted in God's plan to reclaim the fallen creation and renew it. But if creation is to be reconstituted, that renovated new creation must be co-extensive with the old. In other words, it must include all the varieties of creational diversity in human life, including infancy. This means covenant infants must be open to receiving salvation in infancy. They are not beyond God's reach. Nothing hinders the Spirit from working faith in them.

2.  The children of believers share in the faith of their parents. Covenant parents are called to believe the gospel on behalf of their child, but also the child himself becomes a believer through the promises of the covenant. Faith spreads from the parents to the child as the Spirit flows out through the family's organic, covenantal bonds. Obviously, much here is hidden in the secret working of God (as Calvin said), but somehow the Spirit works to connect the faith of the parents to the faith of the child. Faith is not just an individual reality, but also corporate. In the gospels, parental faith procures

blessings for children quite frequently, and paedofaith is simply an application and extension of this principle. Parents who believe the gospel for the sake of their children may be assured that their young children are believers too. There is every reason to believe God rewards parental faith by blessing their children with faith. This is why the children of the God-fearing man are called an inheritance and blessing from the Lord.

3. Infant faith is normative and typical. There is no reason to doubt the presence of infant faith in children who belong to healthy Christian families and churches. In apostate church and family situations we can be far less confident, of course. Nevertheless, in any "normal" situation, the Bible gives us a paedofaith paradigm (e.g., David) through which the developing experiences of our children should be viewed. This means revivalism, however necessary it may have been in countering nominalism and deadness in eighteenth and nineteenth century churches, is itself a very serious distortion of biblical teaching. It is urgent that the church recover a biblically based paedofaith/paedobaptism-grounded approach to parenting so that we can begin countering the influences of our secular culture from the earliest days of our children's lives.

4. Infant faith, along with the covenant promises and the command of Christ, provides a more than adequate grounding for the practice of infant baptism. Infant faith means children can and do make right use of baptism. In principle, *all baptism should be "believer's baptism."* Because covenant children have faith, there is no reason to doubt that their baptisms "took." There is every reason to believe they received what God offers in baptism. There are at least a couple possible errors we should avoid here. Baptism is not constituted by faith; rather, it is offered to faith. Nor does baptism elicit faith; rather, it presupposes faith, and increases, strengthens, confirms, and assures faith.

5. Because of paedofaith and the efficacy of paedobaptism, covenant children should be regarded and treated as Christians. Parents

should welcome and receive their children in Christ's name, meaning the children are regarded as bearers of Christ's presence and in union with Him. Parents should prize and care for their covenant offspring as they would treasure and treat Christ Himself. Parents should disciple their children, nurturing them in the faith and the fear of the Lord. This also means parents should be diligent in cultivating habits and virtues in their children that will enable them to walk worthy of the calling they have received in the gospel. Parents do not need to be anxious or uncertain about the status of their children or God's intentions toward their children, but should live by faith in the promises.

6. The covenant state and status of our children also indicates they should be included at the Lord's Table. Just as children were participants in the sacramental life of the old covenant, including the meals and feasts, so it should be in the new covenant. Paedocommunion is another form of covenant nurture. Because our children have faith, they can receive the body and blood of Christ in the bread and wine. They are part of the body of Christ and should not be excluded just because of their youthful immaturity.

7. Covenant infants have faith, which means *all* who die in infancy are most certainly saved. Grieving Christian parents should be given this solid comfort. However, this is not to say that our children are guaranteed an unconditional salvation if they grow up to reject the covenant. Infant faith is defectible. If covenant children stumble and fall away from the faith, their precious covenantal blessings will become intensified covenantal curses. Their baptism will devolve from waters of life into waters of death and drowning. They will receive the greater condemnation. Furthermore, those through whom offenses come will be judged as well. Jesus said those who turn "little believers" away from Christ will have millstones wrapped around their necks and will be cast into the deepest parts of the sea.

8. Infant faith is mysterious. We are not told how God works faith in the hearts of covenant infants. However, we can insist that God's freedom to work in our children (or the senile or mentally handicapped) is not bounded by our rational and emotional abilities. The gospel is especially for the weak, humble, and poor. Our children are among the best illustrations of gospel grace because their weakness, dependence, and inability are so utterly obvious. Covenant children in home and church are living parables of the gospel for the whole community to see.

9. Infant faith is a matter of relational trust. As a matter of relationship, this faith will grow over time, and as infant believers mature, rational and volitional elements (knowledge of and assent to gospel propositions) will get added into their faith. They believe as infants in order to grow into understanding as adults. But in the meantime, their faith is genuine. Paedofaith is real, authentic faith. It is simply "baby faith." Or, to put it another way, paedofaith is to adult faith what babies are to adults. Paedofaith is not merely a disposition to faith or a potential faith or an openness to faith in the future; it is faith appropriate to the personhood of the child.

10. Paedofaith has a long and venerable theological history. The church fathers were certainly open to a doctrine of paedofaith (and often paedocommunion), and many who grew up in covenant homes claimed to have served God from infancy. Going back to the Reformation, Luther advocated a very strong paedofaith position. Calvin followed suit, adding nuances, but still insisting that infant "seed" faith is real faith. Later, scholastics and Puritans began to qualify and minimize paedofaith in various ways, which in some measure further opened the door to both Enlightenment rationalism and American revivalism. But after a temporary eclipse, the doctrine of paedofaith is making a comeback in several theological traditions, often bringing along with it a pro-paedocommunion movement. Finally, contemporary paedofaith advocates are very interested in exploring non-cognitive, non-discursive ways in which we acquire knowledge. While no doctrine is to be based on

extra-Scriptural considerations, the teaching of Scripture is often clarified and buttressed by these considerations. That seems to be happening, at least in small ways, with the biblical doctrine of paedofaith.

# bibliographic essays

## Chapter Four

*Infants Dying in Infancy*

There are many works on the topic of infants dying in infancy, some more pastoral, others more theological. For a positive account of infant salvation from within the Reformed tradition, see Lewis Bevens Schenck, *The Presbyterian Doctrine of Children in the Covenant* (New Haven: Yale University Press, 1940). Schenck writes, "The Reformed church has *always* believed, on the basis of God's immutable promise, that all children of believers dying in infancy were saved" (118, emphasis added). Schenck argues that this confidence in the Reformed tradition, until the rise of revivalism, was based upon the structure of the covenant and the words of Jesus. This was certainly the view of Luther and Calvin. Schenck's work is really a more comprehensive study of covenant nurture and a critique of American revivalism, but any pastor who has to deal with the issue of infant death and salvation should be sure to read it. It is an outstanding work, perhaps the best ever written on these subjects.

A far less satisfying account is found in R. A. Webb, *The Theology of Infant Salvation* (Richmond, VA: Presbyterian Committee of Publication, 1907). Webb rightly points out that only on Calvinistic principles is it even possible to contemplate the salvation of those who are called out of this world in their infancy. However, Webb denies the possibility of infant faith, suggests an age of accountability, ignores the added comfort provided to the parents by baptism if the child lived long enough to receive the sacrament, and draws no distinction between infants belonging to believers and those who do not. Basically, Webb disconnects the question of infant salvation from the entire covenantal apparatus of Scripture, a bewildering move for a Presbyterian to make.

The same problems (minus an overt age of accountability) are found in B. B. Warfield's discussion of infant salvation in "The Development of the Doctrine of Infant Salvation" in *The Works of Benjamin B. Warfield: Volume 9: Studies in Theology* (Grand Rapids: Baker Book House, 1991 reprint), 411ff. Warfield's historical survey is helpful, but he fails to exegetically ground his view of "uncovenanted mercies" for non-Christians who die in infancy. We are free to be hopeful on this point, but not certain.

A contemporary restatement of the Webb-Warfield position, but in a more pastorally useful form, is Ronald Nash's *When A Baby Dies* (Grand Rapids, MI: Zondervan, 1999). Nash's work is a good resource for someone who wants to know what the issues are and how various Christian traditions have wrestled with them. His work is somewhat hampered by deficient sacramental and covenant theology, but it is still a resource worth consulting.

Another more recent and far more negative study is Edmund R. McDavid III, *Infant Salvation and the Age of Accountability: What Does the Bible Teach* (Birmingham, AL: Hope Publishing, 2003). While McDavid is to be commended for firmly rejecting an age of accountability doctrine, his discussion of infant salvation is vitiated by a total lack of covenant theology. McDavid completely severs God's sovereign election from the administration of the covenant promises, leaving grieving Christian parents with no hope whatsoever for their lost child. In this book, God is presented in raw sovereignty, making Him appear arbitrary, impersonal, and even tyrannical. In truth, God's sovereignty cannot be divorced from His love because His rule is exercised precisely in loving service toward His creation (and even more precisely in cruciform service to His people). Christians should not contemplate the sovereignty of God apart from Christ and the covenant. McDavid's book misses the mark.

## Chapter Six
### *Paedofaith in Protestant History*
There are too many contemporary discussions of paedofaith to catalogue. Here, we will only index some of the more important works favorable to infant faith. Geoffrey Bromiley's *Sacramental Teaching and Practice in the Reformation Churches* (Grand Rapids: Eerdmans, 1957), 53–54, includes a helpful discussion on infant faith. Bromiley argues that Anabaptists led the way in rejecting paedofaith by moving toward semi-Pelagianism. They subjectivized and rationalized the faith, turning baptism into a work of man rather than a gift of God. By denying infants

the possibility of faith, they also eventually ended up denying infants are sinners before they reach an age of moral ability/accountability.

*The Biblical Doctrine of Baptism: A Study Document issued by the Special Commission on Baptism of the Church of Scotland* (Edinburgh: Saint Andrew Press, 1958) includes a helpful discussion of the faith of the church, the faith of the parents, and the faith of the infant. With regard to the last of these, the document states (61):

> Jesus Himself received little children, and there can be no ground for supposing they did not there and then in some measure respond to His love. From the earliest days of infancy a child responds to stimuli, and particularly to the loving care of its mother . . . If a child responds to his mother's care, may he not respond also to the care of God?

The mother's care is not just an analogy for divine care; it is one of the means through which God's nurture of the child is actually carried out. The document goes on to locate the faith of infants in Christ Himself, such that they share in His response of faith to the heavenly Father's faithfulness. Union with Christ is what makes it possible for us to speak of infant faith.

Vern Poythress has written two outstanding articles that impinge on the question of infant faith: "Indifferentism and Rigorism in the Church: With Implications for Baptizing Small Children," *Westminster Theological Journal* 59 (1997), 13–29, and "Linking Small Children with Infants in the Theology of Baptizing," *Westminster Theological Journal* 59 (1997), 143–58. Poythress offers many helpful thoughts on the nature of faith in small children (e.g., "Indifferentism," 18–19) and the way in which faith grows toward maturity in the context of the church ("Linking Small Children," 143ff). Poythress acknowledges that the faith of the immature and inarticulate differs from that found in mature adults ("Linking Small Children," 157), but infant faith is possible because we are saved by grace, not intellectual comprehension. Adjusting expectations to the nature of a person's maturity level is an application of Christian love. Thus, we can be generous in evaluating infants and children without lapsing into laxity. The faith of children is no less genuine simply because it depends primarily upon their parents. Poythress discusses the faith of infants in relation to the faith of their parents and church on pages 144ff, suggesting that their faith, no matter how immature, should not be dismissed. While Poythress does not explicitly connect his arguments with paedocommunion, he shows that children belonging to Christian families are part of the ecclesial assembly and have access to the heavenly sanctuary (150ff). Poythress refutes the notion of an age of accountability on pages 156–57.

Preston Graham's book *A Baptism That Saves: The Reformed, Sacramental Doctrine of Baptism Argued and Applied* (New Haven, CT: Christ Presbyterian Church, 1999) makes several helpful points about infant salvation, the nature of baptism, and the faith of infants. Graham argues that our children are "insiders" to the covenant. He makes a case that baptism is a salvific transaction for elect children, even going so far as to say that "true faith is being given in baptism." Baptism is not the "drama of decision" but the "drama of effectual calling." If your child happens to perish in childhood, "you will be encouraged to know that his or her salvation did not rest upon their own decision . . . Rather, you will know that their election is made sure by the decision God made for them, a decision that began with their being brought into the Church by Christian baptism." Graham also demonstrates that we need to drop our unhealthy preoccupation with individual salvation and recover the biblical emphasis on corporate identity with Christ. Baptism is not merely a private event, but a public sign that puts Spiritual distance between our children and the world.

Because God works salvation instrumentally through baptism, we should raise our children accordingly, forming them into mature disciples of Christ. Graham reminds us we are training Christians, not pagans. He explains:

> Surely the Reformed doctrine of baptism is "good news" for parents. For when we see God bring our child to Christian baptism, this in itself is an evidence that God *is* at work in your children—something that you will countless times remember through the course of their development. When that accident happens—you will remember that God is at work in your child. When that rebellion begins to emerge as from their fallen natures, you will remember that God is at work in your child. Sure, you will want to

steward these situations in such a way as to direct your child to God and His means of grace in prayer, word, and sacrament. But you will take courage to know that nothing happens to your child that God has not decreed. And the promise you cling to is that these things are for good, not evil, to those called by God.

To train a covenant child is to assume the covenant itself as related to your child. You are training a Christian, not a pagan. While you and I are acutely aware of the presence of original sin such that training is necessary as related to Christian discipleship, we are not training someone who is without faith, at least this is not our driving assumption. Their faith may be small. Their faith may be immature. Their faith may at times be shaken. But we are training them as covenant children who by God's grace are being renewed by the power of God that works within them. And this will make a huge difference in the way we train our children.

So, for instance, the child's motivation is the grace of God, not the fear of God's judgment . . . In training a child, we are training them to respond to the grace of God, not out of a desire to escape the judgment of God, but because in Christ they have been graciously passed through the judgment of God that awaits them.

Graham insists that we teach our children faith and repentance, but in the same way that we teach Christians these things, "assuming in them the ability given to them by God to do this." In this way we demonstrate to them that forgiveness of sins is the precondition of obedience. We do not treat them as if they still need to become Christians.

Graham goes on to distinguish sharply the unconfirmed faith of a small child from more mature, confirmed faith in adults. While he provides some excellent thoughts on parental nurture in the context of paedofaith and paedobaptist assumptions, I think his unconfirmed/confirmed distinction rests on very dubious biblical grounds. This is probably not the best way to distinguish paedofaith from adult faith. He fails to note the social/relational core common to faith at every age.

Finally, Bryan Chapell, while not mentioning infant faith per se, speaks of faith germinating and growing in extremely young covenant children as they receive nurture and discipline from their parents and church community. In his essay "A Pastoral Overview of Infant Bap-

tism" in *The Case for Covenantal Infant Baptism* (Phillipsburg, NJ: Presbyterian and Reformed, 2003), edited by Gregg Strawbridge, 26, he writes:

> In this atmosphere, faith naturally germinates and matures so *that*
> *it is possible, even common, for the children of Christian parents never to*
> *know a day that they do not believe that Jesus is their Savior and Lord.*
> Such covenantal growth of a child is, in fact, the normal Christian
> life that God intends for His people, and it is one of the most strik-
> ing, but infrequently mentioned, reasons that baptism is adminis-
> tered to infants.

Children who grow up in a context of faith cannot help but have faith
themselves. They are enveloped by the faith at every turn. They are
predisposed to trust what their parents trust and to believe the teaching
they receive from their elders.

In view of Chapell's words, I cannot help but think here of Cornelius Van Til's remark about his childhood growing up in a Dutch Reformed home: "Though there were no tropical showers of revivals, the
relative humidity was always very high . . . I was 'conditioned' in the
most thorough fashion. I *could not help believing in God*—in the God of
Christianity—in the God of the Bible!" From *Why I Believe in God* (Phila-
delphia: Great Commission Publications, no date), 3–4.

### Chapter Eight
*Paedofaith and the Task of Christian Parenting*
For more on covenantal nurture, see William Evans' "A Tale of Two Pie-
ties: Nurture and Conversion in American Christianity" in *Reformation
and Revival Journal*, Summer 2004 (vol. 13, no. 4), 61–75. Evans compares
nurturing models of piety to those that are more conversion/experience
centered, pointing out strengths and weaknesses of each. Nominalism is a
constant threat in churches that practice the nurture model, but this style
of piety is clearly rooted in the catholic and Reformed tradition. The
conversionist model is a uniquely American form of piety, focusing on
one's psychological experience of the gospel in a decisive and self-
conscious transition from unbelief to faith. The experience is "narratable," and thus giving a compelling "testimony" becomes the mark of
saving grace. While this view is commended for emphasizing our need

for an experience of God's grace, it is highly subjective, individualistic, and encourages an "episodic" view of the Christian life, moving from one mountaintop to another, rather than a consistent "walk" of faithfulness.

Robert Rayburn's excellent paper "The Presbyterian Doctrines of Covenant Children, Covenant Nurture, and Covenant Succession" (available at http://www.faithtacoma.org/covenant2.htm) is extremely important as a historical and theological study. Rayburn shows that the Reformed church has traditionally held to a strong doctrine of covenant succession. The covenant promises serve to comfort parents and lay the groundwork for nurturing children in the life of the kingdom. Rayburn is especially interested in emphasizing the Bible's positive connection between faithful nurture and children who grow to mature faith (though he also touches on the shadow of this doctrine, namely, parental responsibility and blame for children who grow up to rebel against the gospel). His thesis is that Scripture describes the family as the primary means of growing the kingdom through raising up godly offspring; God has determined that grace run in lines of generations, sustained through parental faith and diligence. The typical covenant child will grow up as a believer and a full church member. His argument is that the classical Reformed doctrine of covenant succession and Christian nurture was largely displaced in the American Presbyterian church by the revivalist requirement of an experience of abrupt, conscious conversion. This led to a corresponding alteration in the status of covenant children which has been for the worse. A study of Rayburn's paper reveals just how deeply revivalism has penetrated contemporary Presbyterianism. Rayburn especially laments the fact that the church lets so many baptized children walk away from the faith without any attempts at formal correction or discipline, revealing that we never really believed they were members anyway. A couple paragraphs will have to suffice as a taste of this most excellent work:

> The immensely important consequence of this infant membership is that the duty of parents and the church becomes, thereby, to train their children to believe, feel, and live as becomes the children of God and members of His household, which they are! Especially parents, who are the masters of their children's thoughts in the formative years, are responsible to ensure that the children of

the covenant grow up fully aware and appreciative of the promises which have been made to them by name and the summons
which was issued to them at the headwaters of their lives. Surely
one of the most dismal evidences of the debasement of this doctrine in Presbyterian churches is in the general insensibility of
covenant children themselves to their status, their breathtaking
privileges, and their sacred obligations.

The spiritual culture of their children, their instruction in the
works and will of God, their preparation for a life of faith is made
the direct responsibility of the church's parents according to a great
many texts (Gen. 18:19; Ex. 10:12; 12:24–27; 13:8; 14:16; 31:12–13;
Deut. 4:9; 6:49; Ps. 44:1; 78:18; Isa. 38:19; 2 Tim. 3:14–15). The entirety
of Proverbs is illustration both of the manner and substance of that
covenantal nurture (the covenantal name of God is used throughout
the book). According to Scripture the covenant home is to be both a
school of faith and a temple in which the acknowledgment of God
and His worship confirm and adorn the instruction (cf. Ps. 118:15;
2 Sam. 6:20). The larger community of faith and especially the ministry also bear responsibility for this nurture of mind and heart
(Hos. 4:6; Mic. 2:9; Jer. 2:8–9; 2 Chron. 24:2, 26:5; cf. Zech. 11:16).

For an older, but still relevant work, see John Williamson Nevin's
*The Anxious Bench, Antichrist, and the Sermon on Christian Unity* (Eugene,
OR: Wipf and Stock Publishers, reprint). Nevin gives a devastating critique of the revivalistic system that was arising in his own day. He argues for children "growing up in the bosom of the Church" as the norm
and rejects the quest for a "cheap conversion in a revival." He compares
the system of the "bench" (altar calls) with its "boilerplate conversions"
to the more organic nurture of the "catechesis" model, in which Christian piety is inculcated over time through participation in the life of the
church and familial patterns of piety. Perhaps Nevin's greatest strength
is that he does not root covenant nurture exclusively in domestic life,
but maintains the centrality of the church, even in the discipleship of
children. He does not romanticize about the family, but sees the family's
hope of corporate redemption as grounded in its membership in the
supernatural church family. Parental efforts amount to nothing apart
from the external means of grace offered in the church.

Further, see Hughes Oliphant Old, *The Shaping of the Reformed Baptismal Rite in the Sixteenth Century*, 130ff. Old looks at covenant nurture

through the lens of paedobaptism. He shows that the Reformers advocated a nurturing, covenant-based model of parenting rather than the crisis-conversion model of the Anabaptists and later revivalists. Old's scholarship on these questions is impeccable, and his linking of paedobaptism, paedofaith, and covenant nurture in a package is very helpful.

Though from a somewhat liberal theological perspective, Horace Bushnell's *Christian Nurture* (1847, repr., Cleveland: Pilgrim Press, 1994) remains a classic. When first published in 1847, the work was so strongly opposed that publication had to be temporarily suspended! Even though Charles Hodge disagreed with much of Bushnell's work, he admitted the book was bound to do far more good than evil. Bushnell argued for a domestic alternative to spasmodic revivals, focusing especially on the comprehensive care given by mothers—the touch, the tone of voice, the constant provision of a loving environment—as the key to the child's growth into a mature Christian. Bushnell argued against revivalism's morphology of conversion, suggesting that if our children are sinners, it is never too early to begin seeking to remedy this by teaching them the good. Even very young children can be taught to make pleasing God their way of life. Further, Bushnell argues that the "revivalistic impulse" in American Christianity, beginning with the later Puritans but reaching its zenith in the Second Great Awakening, has produced the belief that children can only become Christians after having spent some time in hatred of the truth as children of wrath, followed by a protracted, intense struggle toward conversion. In other words, only "Hell's Angels"-type testimonies are valid. Against this crisis conversion approach, Bushnell focused on the organic means through which character formation takes place in children over an extended period of time. His emphasis on the "natural" means through which children are molded risked marginalizing their need for "supernatural" grace, and some critics of Bushnell saw this as the soft underbelly of his position. Nevertheless, Bushnell offered a theological rationale for his belief that it was possible and normal for children in Christian homes to grow up Christian, never knowing a day when they were not in God's care. He desired to restore covenant children to their rightful place in the kingdom of God. Bushnell was well ahead of his time in considering the tacit, non-cognitive ways parents can influence and mold children even in their extreme youth. Bushnell's views were controversial even among many who were sympathetic, such as Nevin and Hodge, who accused him of de-supernaturalizing the gospel, church, and sacraments. But his work is a profitable study if read with discernment.

A related work is Candy Gunther Brown's chapter "Domestic Nurture versus Clerical Crisis: The Gender Dimension in Horace Bushnell's and Elizabeth Prentiss's Critiques of Revivalism," a contribution to *Embodying the Spirit: New Perspectives on North American Revivalism* (Baltimore and London: Johns Hopkins Press, 2004), 67–83. Brown provides a handy summary of Bushnell's view of revivalism and covenant nurture as well as the mixed responses offered by Nevin and Hodge. Her point is to show that Bushnell's focus on domestic nurture as an alternative to preacher-driven revivals had the effect of encouraging and empowering women in their domestic tasks as wives and mothers, even in a cultural context in which male headship was still the norm. Brown explores the implications of Bushnell's thesis that the primary responsibility for a child's religious education falls to parents, especially mothers. Religious nurture should not be deferred until the child can have a crisis-like conversion under the ministry of a revivalist preacher. Reliance on revivals practically means that children are trained in sin for years before being taught the good in any aggressive way. In truth, children do not have to feel enmity consciously toward God as preparation for conversion. Indeed, they should grow in obedience and sanctification from their earliest days. The organic connection between parents and children ensures the parents will be incredibly influential in the religious formation of the children for good or ill. Mothers are especially important because of the intensity and frequency of their interaction with their children. Their task is to sanctify the home's time and space so that the child grows up in an environment of holiness. There is no need for a revivalistic crisis orientation; the Holy Spirit's work can be found in day-to-day, ordinary routines. Lifelong growth in holiness rather than sudden and dramatic conversion should be the goal of home life.

Brown's essay also looks at Prentiss's *Stepping Heavenward*, a book that it is still in print (Amityville, NY: Calvary Press Publishing, 1998) and also is worthwhile reading. Bushnell offered to mothers an alternative to simply waiting for clerical-led revivals; he argued that mothers could actually *do* something toward the goal of the child's salvation. Prentiss's book picks up on precisely this theme. While in some ways an overly sentimentalized proto-feminist tract, Prentiss's story also provides a very interesting critique of revivalism from a domestic/maternal nurturing perspective. Prentiss grew up in a revivalist family. Her father thought conversion was a momentous, intense, crisis experience. But Prentiss herself, after experiencing her own revivalistic conversion and then struggling with doubts about salvation for years afterwards, finally moved toward more of a covenant nurture model under the influence of Bushnell. She became very critical of revivalism's tendency to base assurance on fluctuating feelings (which usually waned after the revival was over anyway) and its tendency to create agonizing anxiety in the hearts of young people over their election and regeneration.

In *Stepping Heavenward*, Prentiss tells Katy's fictional story by giving us a record of her diary from youth through marriage and motherhood. Katy's father-in-law represents the harsh revivalism she grew up under. He demands every true Christian be able to give a narrative account of his conversion as a crisis experience. He tells Katy that being a "faithful" parent means telling her four-year-old son he is "in a state of condemnation." He objects to preaching that isn't doctrinal enough and spends most of his time overcome with gloominess. By contrast, Katy's pastor, Dr. Cabot, represents a more orthodox version of Bushnell. He gives the comfort of the gospel even to those who cannot testify to having had a dramatic, emotionally-charged conversion experience and in fact tells Katy that Christian children usually will not be able to remember a time of conversion if their parents have done well. Dr. Cabot tells Katy to get to work pursuing holiness *now* rather than waiting for a revival to strike. Likewise, he counsels parents to nurture their children in the ways of God rather than delaying Spiritual nurture until they experience a revival. According to Dr. Cabot, revivalism causes people either to be over-confident because they think the "great work" has already been done, or to be perpetually in a state of doubt and despair over the condition of their souls because what they thought was the "great work" might not have been authentic. Dr. Cabot tells Katy "life is too precious to spend in a tread-mill" and there is no time to "sit with folded hands waiting for the blessing [of revivalistic experience]." Instead of fretting over salvation, Katy should get to work pursuing holiness—"stepping heavenward"—in her daily life. She should obey even when she doesn't *feel* like it, recognizing that her personal holiness is the single most important factor in her child becoming holy. Katy learns to be neither romantic about her child's innocence nor apathetically awaiting a revival for his sake. Instead, she uses the opportunities presented in daily life to help her child move toward holiness, knowing that her high calling as a mother gave even her smallest words and most mundane actions great impact on others in the home. Sanctification happens as we live godly lives in everyday tasks and relationships. While the book has a slight feminist tinge (especially in overly exaggerating the role of the mothers over the fathers in creating the Spiritual culture of the home), if read with some care, Prentiss's story can yield useful insights.

Pierre Marcel's work on baptism, *The Biblical Doctrine of Infant Baptism: Sacrament of the Covenant of Grace* (London: James Clarke, 1953), translated by Philip Edgcumbe Hughes, includes a section on covenant nurture (229ff). Marcel says the church needs to preach the covenant to parents, and she ought to preach the covenant to children as well. Parents' greatest incentive to nurture their children in the way of the Lord arises from the fact that God has indeed made their children His own from their infancy. While Marcel's discussion is not as robust as it could be, it has the advantage of linking the vocation of Christian parents to their children's baptisms, something that few American theologians have done.

A more recent study of great practical usefulness is Marva Dawn's *Is It a Lost Cause? Having the Heart of God for the Church's Children* (Grand Rapids: Eerdmans, 1997). Dawn provides a wise, winsome, and compassionate look at how the church can be hospitable to her children, receiving them in Christ's name. Dawn's argument, essentially, is that it takes a church to raise a Christian child in today's secularized world. As parents, we must parent by faith, relying on the Holy Spirit, given to us and our children at baptism, to make our efforts at character formation effective. Dawn also points out certain evils our children should be sensitized to, though conservative parents often overlook their danger (in particular, materialism and consumerism).

Edmund Gross' *Will My Children Go to Heaven? Hope and Help for Believing Parents* (Phillipsburg, NJ: Presbyterian and Reformed, 1995) is a very accessible book on these themes. This work is a study of covenant succession, showing that believing parents do not need to be anxious over the salvation of their children. Parents who trust God's promises will not be disappointed. Of course, parental faith also bears fruit, so believing parents will be diligent in prayer, teaching, and discipline. Occasionally Gross lapses into a conversionist mentality, but overall his book is extremely useful. He also includes some very pastoral thoughts on how Christian parents who have "blown it" should seek to reclaim their children for Christ.

Susan Hunt is an evangelical Presbyterian who has written several insightful and helpful books on family issues. Her book *Heirs of the Covenant: Leaving a Legacy of Faith for the Next Generation* (Wheaton, IL: Crossway, 2000) is an excellent study of covenant parenting. Without getting into questions of baptismal efficacy or paedofaith, Hunt makes a compelling biblical, historical, and anecdotal case for covenant succession and draws out many practical implications. While not theologically or exegetically rigorous, her book is a pleasure to read.

No list of family nurture books would be complete without mention of Douglas and Nancy Wilson. See Douglas Wilson, *Standing on the Promises* (Moscow, ID: Canon Press, 1997); *Her Hand in Marriage* (Moscow, ID: Canon Press, 1997); *Fidelity* (Moscow, ID: Canon Press, 1999); and *Future Men* (Moscow, ID: Canon Press, 2001). See also Nancy Wilson, *Praise Her in the Gates* (Moscow, ID: Canon Press, 2000). All of these books are full of practical wisdom, biblical principles, and provocative insights. Occasionally prone to over-simplification, but always driven by a desire to apply the Scriptures to modern life, the Wilsons have given Christian parents a storehouse of edifying literature to help them in their task.

Finally, the collection of essays *The Child in Christian Thought* (Grand Rapids: Eerdmans, 2001), edited by Marcia Bunge, is packed with useful information, generally drawn from historical surveys. The book focuses on the nature of the child as understood in various Christian traditions, and the responsibilities of church, family, and society toward the child. Some essays are not without deep flaws, but the book as a whole still provides much food for thought and reflection. It is especially important for American evangelicals to see how odd their view of children is against the backdrop of the wider Christian tradition.

I would be remiss if I did not mention at least one example of what *not* to do with our children. Here we must be a bit more thorough in our comments. Dennis Gundersen's Reformed Baptist work *Your Child's Profession of Faith* (Amityville, NY: Calvary Press, 1994) is well intentioned and contains many nuggets of biblical truth. But the overall effect of the work is to make parents highly suspicious of the Spiritual experiences and professions of their children. In Gundersen's view the worst possible thing we could do is allow our children to be deceived into thinking they are Christians when they really are not. Giving assurance is a dangerous thing since it leads all too easily to presumption. (Apparently, exasperating our children by making it almost impossible for them to prove their love for Jesus to our satisfaction is no danger at all!) Thus, Gundersen's book attempts to give parents rigorous tests for discerning the validity of their children's professions. He writes, "Being converted requires one to come to the point where he can take a step of independent devotion to Jesus Christ, and this can hardly be recognizable in a young child" (18). Of course, this is pure individualism: our children must be independent and autonomous before they can become Christians. This methodology hardly prepares our children to live as interdependent members of a faith community. Instead, it readies them for a "me and Jesus" kind of piety, cut off from the church family. It sets our children off down a rather unhelpful path.

Gundersen even suggests that after parents have become fairly confident about their child's profession, they should still hold off on baptism for a while just to be safe (50). But, again, this gives the child a totally false understanding of the Christian life. The child's personal exercise of faith is divorced from the sacrament of initiation into the covenant community, as though the church were a mere appendage to an individual's private relationship with Christ.

Gundersen suggests that determining the authenticity of a child's profession is far more difficult than that of an adult. But it is not at all clear why this is the case. Why is it easier to read the heart of an adult than a child? If anything, adults are far more prone to self-deception and hypocrisy since they are so much more psychologically complex.

Adults are far more skilled at "faking it," whereas children tend to have simple, unfeigned authenticity. Besides, while Gundersen catalogs numerous passages that speak of the sinful condition into which our children are born, he does not mention *any* of the biblical passages that speak more positively of our children (e.g., Ps. 22:9–10; Mt. 19:14). He doesn't even touch on the fact that Scripture presents children as models of faith! Instead, he picks out various passages that use childishness metaphorically (e.g., 1 Cor. 14:20; Eph. 4:14) to show that children are untrustworthy when it comes to Spiritual realities. (He ignores the fact that these passages are not necessarily critical of childhood as such, but of childishness *in adults* who should be grown up already. The Bible does not object to five-year-olds who live like five-year-olds; it does rebuke thirty-year-olds who live like five-year-olds!) This is consistent Reformed Baptist theology, refusing to acknowledge any sense in which the children of Christians are distinct from the world, but it is an egregious error nonetheless.

For Gundersen (and for far too many folks of both Reformed Baptist orientation and even Presbyterian persuasion), any attempt at "covenant nurture" is regarded as presumption. It only feeds a false sense of assurance to treat children as believers apart from detecting that they have had a sound conversion experience. Gundersen chides overzealous parents for pressuring their pastors to accept as valid the professions of faith made by their young, untested, intellectually immature children. Parents all too often "show insensitive blindness to the considerable difficulties of being sure that a child's profession of faith is real . . . it will be *a very difficult task for us* to apprise if a child is truly saved" (13, 18). Our children are more impulsive than Peter, so we should never accept their testimony at face value (49–50). Again, Gundersen fails to explain why it is any easier to measure the reality of an adult's profession, or why pastors would know better than parents how the child is doing Spiritually (especially since parents are with the kids on a daily basis). He seems oblivious to the fact that we can never have absolute certainty about the state of *any* other person's heart, whatever their age. Gundersen argues that immature professions are unreliable because children cannot calculate the cost of discipleship and do not really understand the nature of commitment. If a nine-year-old says he intends to follow Jesus his whole life, it would be unwise to accept that testimony at face value (15–16). According to Gundersen, a child disciple may be possible, but if so, it is an extremely rare case.

Besides completely ignoring the Bible's covenantal framework, which includes our children in a favorable relationship with God even from infancy, Gundersen admits no possibility that children can gradually *grow* into the commitments of discipleship over time. He treats discipleship as an all or nothing affair, so that if a child does not *already* fully understand what it means to put Jesus ahead of mother and father, then he cannot be a genuine disciple (cf. Lk. 14:26). But by this hermeneutical logic, one wonders how Gundersen justifies feeding infants, in light of the fact that they do not do any work (cf. 2 Thess. 3:10). The insensitivity of this way of applying the Bible is hard to fathom. It is all rigor and demand, apart from a foundation of grace. Essentially, Gundersen requires our children to grow big and strong without being fed. He insists our children make bricks without straw. This Pharaoh-style parenting demands more than the mere presence of faith; it demands its mature articulation to be counted worthy (36ff). It is hard to square this with *sola fide.*

Gundersen recommends that we practice suspicion toward our children. For example, he uses Proverbs 1:1–4 to demonstrate that our children are naïve and therefore not capable of faith (25ff). But this kind of exegesis confuses *training in wisdom* with *conversion.* Proverbs 1:1–4 could be applied to a brand-new adult convert, with quite a bit of justification. For Gundersen the gospel is really only for the intellectually mature and theologically sophisticated. Thus, childhood is not a time of nurturing in the faith (contra Eph. 6:4), but of patiently waiting until our children get old enough to make their own decision for Christ so that discipleship can begin (31ff).

Gundersen formulates his position in such a way that it is impossible to believe that infants dying in infancy can be saved. He says, "If anyone is saved, he is saved through knowing the truth, and certainly the bare minimum that could be expected of a saved person for a credible profession would be to believe the truths of 1 Corinthians 15:3–4" (40). In other words, if our children cannot grasp the propositional facts of the gospel narrative, they simply cannot be reached by God's grace. Apparently, the gift of faith depends on the development of a mature intellect. Gundersen also requires our children to manifest mature emotional attachment to Jesus in order to make a credible profession of faith (40–41). Gundersen's diagnostic tests for love and faith are so rigorous that if they were applied to familial relationships, we would also have to deny that children can love or trust their parents! If a child is too immature to say "I love Jesus" with meaningful conviction, why is it any different when the child says "I love you, Mommy"? If the former is suspect, why not the latter?

Amazingly, in commenting on the household baptisms in Acts, Gundersen points out that there are no professions of faith by children in the New Testament, as if that bolsters his case (55). He seems oblivious to the covenantal alternative, namely, that children did not have to make independent professions of faith precisely because they were already embraced in the covenantal relationship with their parents. Gundersen tries unconvincingly to evade the household theology of Acts. Further, Gundersen audaciously points out that none of the gospel writers' twenty-two references to children indicate that children became disciples (55–56). But this simply misses the point of the child-centeredness of Jesus' ministry in texts we examined above in chapter two. In Matthew 18:2, Jesus *called* a child to Himself. This sort of call is the essence of an invitation to discipleship. How does the child respond? Unlike many of the adults Jesus called to Himself (e.g., Mt. 19:16–22), this child *comes* to Him. In other words, he responds to the call in faith, in the appropriate way. Jesus then says this child is the model of entering the kingdom. If that is not an endorsement of child discipleship, it is hard to imagine what would suffice.

Further, Paul disciples covenant children in Ephesians 6:1–3 when he applies the Mosaic law to them in its new covenant form. Gundersen thinks our children are commanded to obey because in learning submission to authority they are best prepared to receive Jesus in the future (33–34). But that doesn't match what Paul wrote. Paul tells children to obey their parents *in the Lord* (Eph. 6:1). The command carries with it a *promise* that can only be apprehended by faith (Eph. 6:2–3). Paul is not giving our children a bare "law" to prepare them for future reception of the gospel. He is treating them as full-fledged disciples who need to grow continually in faith and obedience, just like their parents. There is no difference in the way Paul approaches adults and children in the covenant community. Indeed, given that children are addressed by Paul in chapter six as part of the church community, they must also be included in his opening address of the letter. The children, too, are described as saints who were elected in Christ before the dawn of creation in order to be holy and blameless (Eph. 1:1ff).

Of course, the biblical alternative to Gundersen's pessimism about our children has already been sketched out in the preceding pages. Instead of trying to discern whether or not our children "really, really mean it" when they tell us they love Jesus, we should receive and raise our children in accord with the covenant promises. After all, a child's profession may indeed be a murky thing, but the promises of God are crystal clear.

Finally, I would suggest reading two essays in tandem with one another: James B. Jordan's "Conversion," found in his excellent book *The Sociology of the Church: Essays in Reconstruction* (Tyler, TX: Geneva Ministries, 1986), 151–61, and Peter Leithart's eminently practical "Five Maxims for Parents," an article available on the web at http://homepage.ntlworld.com/haylett/fm/fm11_maxims.html. These articles fit together well in that Jordan looks at the stages of conversion a child passes through on his way to mature Christian faith, while Leithart suggests a chronologically unfolding pattern of parental nurture, matched to the child's level of development. The two essays together provide a picture of flexible parental training suited to the unique needs of the child's age and stage in life. Both authors share a common presupposition: human life is not static, but dynamic, and our theology of conversion as well as our practice of parenting must take into account these dynamics.

Jordan identifies four basic types of conversion: the conversion of a total outsider to Christianity; the daily conversion of the Christian from sin to faith; crisis conversions, when a Christian passes through a trial of some sort into deeper maturity; and stage conversions, in which a person's faith is converted into a new form as he moves into a new stage of life. Jordan laments that we have not done justice to these various types of conversion experiences (except the first, which has been absolutized as the only valid model).

Jordan challenges the pietistic notion of conversion, which stresses an inward, sudden, once-and-for-all experience that is narratable and (usually) dateable. Using college students involved in campus ministry as his examples, Jordan points out that these testimonies are so standardized, they are practically a matter of fixed ritual. First, the young person says he thought he was already a Christian; but then (usually under the guidance of an older, influential Spiritual supervisor who is not a parent) he realized that he wasn't *really* a Christian; thus, he gives his life to Christ in a decisive and dramatic way, experiencing "conversion." This seemingly independent decision is regarded as the person's starting point as a "true" Christian.

Jordan gives a number of psychological insights into this phenomenon, showing it is not entirely wrong, though it needs reinterpretation in light of a broader, more biblical understanding of conversion. If we focus everything on a one time conversion event, looking back to that experience rather than moving forward into new "conversions," we get frozen in a state of immaturity. A youthful experience of Christ gets normalized for all of life.

Jordan proceeds to identify a more biblical model of gradual conversion in the life of a covenant child, proceeding through three basic stages toward maturity. First, there is childlike trust in the context of family and church; then a period of adolescence, in which the youth begins to internalize, individualize, and more personally "own" the faith of his childhood; and finally, the mature faith of adulthood, which gives rise to a deeper, more complex, and sober outlook on life.

Leithart's essay uses a finer-grain lens, breaking childhood itself down into three stages. Parents move their children through these stages to adulthood, adjusting their expectations and methods according to the age and stage of the children. At first, parents are *controllers*, governing (by sheer authority) every aspect of the child's life. As the child begins to become more capable (usually around age seven or eight), parents enter into the *coaching* phase. This is a time of testing and training. Children are given responsibilities to see how they handle them. Parents are careful to stretch their children toward independence without overwhelming them. Finally, parents enter the *caring* stage in which they relate to their mature children as fellow adults. They may still give (usually solicited) advice, but for the most part they will regard their children as peers, allowing them to make their own decisions and mistakes. They can intervene when necessary, but such instances should be rare.

As Leithart points out, the problem is that some parents only care when they should control, and when they should be moving into the caring phase, they have to start trying to control out-of-control teenagers. Parents must adapt to their children as they grow, not giving responsibility too early or withholding it for too long. As Leithart says, "Knowing when to tighten and loosen the reins requires a great deal of wisdom and prayer." Indeed. God help us.

# scripture reference index

# *index*